Marriage Records

of

Mecklenburg County Virginia

- 1765-1810 -

By:
Katherine B. Elliott

Southern Historical Press, Inc.
Greenville, South Carolina

Please direct all correspondence and orders to:

www.southernhistoricalpress.com
or
SOUTHERN HISTORICAL PRESS, Inc.
PO BOX 1267
Greenville, SC   29601
southernhistoricalpress@gmail.com

Originally published: South Hill, VA.   1963
Copyright 1963 by: Katherine B. Elliott
Copyright Transferred 1984 to:
    Southern Historical Press, Inc.
ISBN #0-89308-376-3
All rights Reserved.
Printed in the United States of America

FOREWORD

This volume is not a reprint of "Mecklenburg County Marriage Bonds, 1765-1810" which was published in 1928 by Stratton Nottingham. The marriage records in this volume have been copied from the individual marriage bonds and minister's returns in the Clerk's Office of Mecklenburg County.

In addition to the records in the Clerk's Office, the original manuscript copy of the marriage records abstracted by Mr. John Y. Hutcheson in 1924 has been checked. It is unfortunate that many of the marriage records, for both Mecklenburg and Lunenburg Counties before 1782, have not been preserved. An attempt was made to locate all of the marriage records of Mecklenburg County, for the years 1765-1810, which may now be in existence.

An examination of the returns of ministers revealed thirty six marriages for which no bonds could be found. As the marriage records before 1765 were recorded in Lunenburg County, the records were examined to locate all early records applying to Mecklenburg County. Since some marriages of Mecklenburg County residents took place in other counties, the records of Halifax, Charlotte and Brunswick Counties were examined. The records in nearby counties in North Carolina were examined also. The additional records collected have been listed as a supplement to the records in this volume.

This volume is issued as a companion volume to the "Marriage Records, 1811-1853" which was published in 1962. The format followed in compiling this volume is the same as that used in printing the 1811-1853 records.

I acknowledge with appreciation the assistance and the courtesies extended me by Mr. N. G. Hutcheson, Clerk of Mecklenburg County, and his staff. I acknowledge, also, my indebtedness to Mr. John Y. Hutcheson, Boydton, Virginia, for graciously lending me his copy of abstracts of Mecklenburg County marriage records. It was at his suggestion that the compiliation of this volume was undertaken.

Without the assistance and advice of my husband, Herbert A. Elliott, this volume would not have been undertaken by me. He prepared the manuscript copy from which this volume has been printed.

Katherine Blackwell Elliott

CONTENTS

ABERNATHY, Tignal   Martha Holmes
   M.B. May 8, 1796   M. May 12, 1796
   Minister: John Loyd   Surety: John Holmes

ADAMS, Isaac   Judith Carroll
   M.B. December 30, 1786   Surety: William Parish

ADAMS, Jeremiah   Jinsey Redding
   M.B. September 22, 1798   M. October 6, 1798
   Minister: Charles Ogburn   Surety: Drury Creedle
   Note: Jeremiah, son of Thomas and Lucy Adams

ADAMS, Richard   Sally Allen
   M.B. October 28, 1808   M. November 17, 1808
   Minister: James Meacham   Surety: Fielding Noel

ADAMS, Sackfield *   Betsy Daly
   M.B. June 23, 1795   M. August 4, 1795
   Minister: John Loyd   Surety: William Dailey
   * Isaac Field Adams

AKIN, Joseph   Mary Eastland
   M.B. October 10, 1774   Surety: William Eastland

ALDRIDGE, John   * Agnes Baugh
   M.B. January 20, 1800   M. January 22, 1800
   Minister: Ebenezer Macgowan   Surety: E. Macgowan
   * Widow of James Baugh

ALEXANDER, Mark   Lucy Bugg
   M.B. May 20, 1789   Surety: Samuel Goode
   Minister: Thomas Scott
   Note: Lucy, daughter of Jacob and Marjery Bugg

ALEXANDER, Mark   Elizabeth Q. McHarg
   M.B. January 19, 1797   M. January 26, 1797
   Minister: John Loyd   Surety: Robert Baskervill

ALEXANDER, Mark   Nancy Eaton
   M.B. October 18, 1804   Surety: William Baskervill

ALLEN, Arva   Polly Clarke
   M.B. August 1, 1786   M. August 19, 1786
   Minister: John Marshall   Surety: Bolling Clarke

ALLEN, Charles   Sarah Smith
   M.B. April 28, 1781   Surety: David Royster
   Consent: Drury Smith, father of Sarah

ALLEN, Ephraim   Patsey Skelton
    M.B. February 13, 1792   Surety: Thomas Allen
    Minister: James Read

ALLEN, Darling   Judith Nance
    M.B. May 19, 1783   Surety: Robert Nance
    Note: Darling Allen, son of William Allen

ALLEN, Gray   Molly Nance
    M.B. December 16, 1791   Surety: William Drumwright
    Consent: Robert Nance, father of Molly
    Consent: Darling Allen, brother of Gray
    Note: Gray Allen, son of William Allen

ALLEN, James   Frances Comer
    M.B. April 13, 1795   M. April 15, 1795
    Minister: William Richards   Surety: Burwell Russell

ALLEN, John   Nancy Morgain
    M.B. December 15, 1783   Surety: Frederick Rainey
    Note: John Allen, son of William Allen

ALLEN, John   Elizabeth Bugg
    M.B. October 3, 1791   M. October 6, 1791
    Minister: Edward Almand   Surety: Thomas Langley
    Note: John Allen of Buckingham County

ALLEN, John   Patsey Cox
    M.B. January 14, 1793   M. January 22, 1793
    Minister: William Creath   Surety: Thomas Cox

ALLEN, John   Martha Colley
    M.B. November 12, 1798   M. December 22, 1798
    Minister: Charles Ogburn   Surety: William Brown

ALLEN, John   Constant Marriott
    M.B. March 3, 1806   Surety: Thomas Marriott

ALLEN, Jones   Nancy Lewis
    M.B. January 8, 1810   Surety: Robert Lewis

ALLEN, Matthew   Mary Brawner
    M.B. May 8, 1797   Surety: James Thompson

ALLEN, Meredith   Nancy Cooper
    M.B. August 9, 1788   Surety: John Bailey
    Consent: William Allen, father of Meredith

ALLEN, Pleasant   Rebeccah Watson
    M.B. August 8, 1787   Surety: John Allen
    Consent: William Allen, Senr., father of Pleasant

ALLEN, Richard   Elizabeth B. Blacketter
    M.B. November 6, 1809   Surety: David Blacketter

ALLEN, Robert Jones   Caty Hollins
    M.B. December 1, 1786   Surety: Thomas Richardson

ALLEN, Ruel   Mary Pulliam
    M.B. January 13, 1794   M. January 21, 1794
    Minister: William Creath   Surety: James Norment

ALLEN, Thomas   Lucy Adams
    M.B. December 13, 1796   M. December 22, 1796
    Minister: William Richards   Surety: John Freeman

ALLEN, Young   Sarah Poole
    M.B. February 27, 1786   Surety: Darling Allen
    Note: Young Allen, son of William Allen

ALLGOOD, Edward   Elizabeth Hudson
    M.B. November 28, 1788   Surety: Bartlett Cox

ALLGOOD, George   Dicey Hudson
    M.B. January 23, 1806   Surety: Thomas Mallett
    Minister: William Richards   M. January 29, 1806

ALLGOOD, Jeremiah   Dicey Harris
    M.B. December 13, 1802   M. December 20, 1802
    Minister: Edward Almand   Surety: James Harris
    Note: Dicey Harris, daughter of James Harris

ALLGOOD, John   Jinsey Blake
    M.B. December 31, 1798   M. January 3, 1799
    Minister: William Creath   Surety: Edward Goodrich

ALLGOOD, Samuel   Mary Royal
    M.B. October 4, 1786   Surety: Edward Clarke

ALLGOOD, Samuel   Jinny Claunch
    M.B. December 29, 1804   Surety: Matthew Claunch

ALLGOOD, William   Sarah Royal
    M.B. March 5, 1790   Surety: Manley Allgood

ALSTON, John   Jane H. Davis
    M.B. December 14, 1799   M. December 19, 1799
    Minister: Ebenezer Macgowan   Surety: Thomas H. Davis

ANDERSON, Charles   Sally Thornton
    M.B. September 11, 1787   Surety: James Thornton
    Note: Charles Anderson of Amelia County

ANDERSON, Jordan   Margaret Easter
    M.B. June 6, 1785   Surety: Lewis Rolfe
    Note: Jordan Anderson of Prince Edward County

ANDERSON, Joseph   Martha Edmondson
    M.B. August 12, 1794   Surety: William Phillips
    Minister: William Creath

ANDREWS, Ephraim, Junr.   Stacy Humphress
    M.B. February 15, 1786   Surety: Thomas Humphress

ANDREWS, Thomas   Margaret Broadfoot
    M.B. March 29, 1791   Surety: Frederick Andrews

APPERSON, David   Martha Speed
    M.B. May 30, 1778   Surety: Richard Hanserd

APPERSON, Samuel   Polly Worsham
    M.B. October 1, 1801   Surety: Archibald Clarke
    Consent: John Worsham, father of Polly

APPERSON, Thomas   Kitty Wynn
    M.B. August 6, 1791   M. August 12, 1791
    Minister: James Read   Surety: Holeman Rice

ARMISTEAD, John   Elizabeth Royster
    M.B. July 17, 1777   John Farrar
    Consent: William Royster, father of Elizabeth

ARNOLD, Isaac   Anne Andrews
    M.B. May 16, 1795   M. May 21, 1795
    Minister: Charles Ogburn
                   Surety: George Hightower Walker
    Consent: George Andrews   Consent: John Arnold

ARNOLD, Joseph   Frances Drumwright
    M.B. September 24, 1800   Surety: William Drumwright

ARRINGTON, John   Susanna Vaughan
    M.B. April 30, 1790
    Note: Married in Granville County, N. C.

ASHTON, Henry   Elizabeth Hanner Barbara Watts
    M.B. March 31, 1788   Surety: Richard Watts
    Minister: Thomas Scott

ATKINS, Thomas   Sally Johnston
    M.B. January 8, 1810   Surety: Caleb Johnston

ATKINSON, Arthur C.   Elizabeth Pinson
    M.B. September 12, 1791   M. September 29, 1791
    Minister: James Read   Surety: Thomas Pinson

AVERETT, Thomas   Rebecca Allen
    M.B. July 13, 1807   M. July 23, 1807
    Minister: William Richards   Surety: Joel Averett

AVERY, Joel   Franky Puryear
    M.B. December 12, 1808   M. December 29, 1808
    Minister: William Richards   Surety: Elijah Puryear

AVERY, Matthew   Obedience Crowder
    M.B. September 12, 1803   Surety: John Wagstaff
    Minister: William Richards

AVORY, Brown   Elizabeth Royster
    M.B. January 27, 1810   Surety: Miles Hall

AVORY, Elijah Evans   Delia Crew
    M.B. June 12, 1809   Surety: Leeman Haile

AVORY, James   Polly Spain
    M.B. December 12, 1808   M. December 20, 1808
    Minister: William Richards   Surety: Abraham Reamy

AVORY, Jarrott   Rebecca Worsham
    M.B. December 17, 1810   Surety: Daniel Jones

BAGWELL, Samuel   Catherine Brown
    M.B. November 12, 1788   Surety: Richard Edmondson
    Note: Samuel Bagwell of Brunswick County

BAILEY, Benjamin   Patsy Durham
    M.B. June 11, 1798   M. June 28, 1798
    Minister: William Richards
                        Surety: Valentine McCutcheon

BAILEY, George   Duannar Hicks
    M.B. October 21, 1799   Surety: Bartholomew Medley
    Minister: William Creath

BAILEY, Henry   Polly Edwards
    M.B. December 9, 1793   Surety: Thomas Edwards
    Consent: John Edwards, father of Polly

BAILEY, Henry   Jessie Curtis
    M.B. February 17, 1802   Surety: Jesse Curtis

BAILEY, Howard   Elizabeth Vaughan
    M.B. December 3, 1783   Surety: John Bell

BAILEY, John   Anne Allen
    M.B. March 2, 1791   M. March 5, 1791
    Minister: Henry Ogburn   Surety: Elisha Arnold

BAILEY, Peter   Sarah Baker
    M.B. August 27, 1792   Surety: Thomas Jeffries
    Minister: William Creath
    Note: Sarah, daughter of Zachariah and Jane Baker

BAILEY, Richard   Anne Brown
    M.B. January 12, 1795   Surety: William Brown

BAILEY, William   Martha Holloway
    M.B. November 21, 1801   Surety: Henry Bailey

BAIRD, Charles W.   Fanny D. Gregory
    M.B. December 6, 1808   Surety: West Gregory
    Consent: Richard Gregory, father of Fanny

BAIRD, John   Sally Cunningham
    M.B. May 3, 1805   Surety: Jesse Johnson

BAIRD, William   Sylvia Bass
    M.B. November 29, 1802   M. December 1, 1802
    Minister: James Meacham   Surety: Independence Poarch

BAKER, James   Polly Holmes
    M.B. October 4, 1804   Surety: Richard Crowder

BAKER, William   Leah Hendrick
    M.B. May 12, 1800   M. May 17, 1800
    Minister: Matthew Dance   Surety: George Baker

BAPTIST, Matthew   Aphia W. Clausel
    M.B. December 11, 1809   Surety: Benjamin W. Jeffries
    Minister: George Micklejohn

BARBER, Edward   Jincey Williamson
    M.B. December 9, 1799   Surety: James Greenwood
    Consent: Robert Williamson, father of Jincey

BARKER, Charles   Barbara Walton
    M.B. August 15, 1791   M. August 18, 1791
    Minister: James Read   Surety: John Walton
    Note: Charles Barker of Nottoway County

BARNER, Harrison   Polly Jones
    M.B. May 17, 1786   Surety: Theophilus Harrison

BARNES, Brackett   Jane Jeffries
    M.B. May 8, 1797   M. May 11, 1797
    Minister: William Richards
                         Surety: Swepson Jeffries, Sr.

BARNES, John   Rebecca Winkfield
    M.B. January 15, 1794   M. January 23, 1794
    Minister: John Loyd   Surety: Joshua Winkfield
    Note: John Barnes of Brunswick County

BARNES, Phillip   Mary White
    M.B. January 8, 1798   M. January 20, 1798
    Minister: William Richards   Surety: William Naish

BARNETT, John   Sally Merryman
    M.B. August 7, 1805   Surety: Richard Hailey

BARNETT, Thomas   Hannah Rook
    M.B. June 10, 1790   Surety: William Walker
    Consent: Anna Thompson, relation not stated

BARNETT, William   Judith Thomason
    M.B. January 10, 1793   M. January 15, 1793
    Minister: John Loyd   Surety: William Bowen

BARRON, John   Charlotte Watson
    M.B. December 2, 1809   Surety: James Standley

BARROW, William   Susannah Marshall
    M.B. October 2, 1801   Surety: Dennis Marshall
    Minister: John Phaup   M. October 22, 1801
    Note: Susannah, daughter of Samuel Marshall

BARRY, James Harwell   Patsy Thompson
    M.B. January 20, 1808   Surety: William Crow

BARRY, Jóseph   Mary Massey
    M.B. December 30, 1795   M. December 31, 1795
    Minister: Matthew Dance   Surety: Drury Andrews
    Consent: Thomas and Mary Massey, parents of Mary

BASEY, Jesse *   Jane Perrin Giles
    M.B. December 19, 1791   M. December 21, 1791
    Minister: John Loyd   Surety: Isham Eppes
    Consent: Henry Edward Giles, father of Jane
    * Jesse Baisey

BASKERVILL, Edward   Susannah Holmes
    M.B. March 4, 1800   M. March 5, 1800
    Minister: Ebenezer Macgowan   Surety: John Dortch
    Note: Susannah, daughter of Samuel Holmes

BASKERVILL, George H.   Elizabeth Tabb
    M.B. December 16, 1791   Surety: Robert Baskervill
    Minister: John Loyd
    Note: George Hunt, son of George Baskervill

BASKERVILL, John   Martha Burton
    M.B. July 30, 1765   Surety: Samuel Young
    Note: John, son of George Baskervill

BAUGH, Daniel   Lucy Brooks
    M.B. October 10, 1780   Surety: John Eppes

BAUGH, James   Peggy Smith
    M.B. December 22, 1800   M. December 31, 1800
    Minister: Ebenezer Macgowan   Surety: John Smith, Jr.
    Consent: John Smith, Senr., father of Peggy

BAUGH, Richard   Elizabeth P. Harwell
    M.B. May 28, 1800   Surety: Edward Patrick Davis
    Minister: Ebenezer Macgowan
    Consent: James Harwell, father of Elizabeth

BAUGH, William B.   Martha Minge Bilbo
    M.B. November 15, 1804   Surety: William Baskervill
    Consent: John and Agnes Aldridge
    Note: William Batte, son of James Baugh, deceased
    Note: Agnes Baugh, mother, married (2) John Aldridge

BEASLEY, James   Rebecca Jones
    M.B. September 10, 1800   Surety: Uriah Hawkins
    Minister: Ebenezer Macgowan

BEASLEY, John   Martha N. Insco
    M.B. June 15, 1801   Surety: William Insco

BEASLEY, Thomas   Sally Jackson
    M.B. December 22, 1800   M. December 26, 1800
    Minister: Ebenezer Macgowan   Surety: Mark L. Jackson

BEASLEY, William   Rebecca Vaughan
    M.B. May 19, 1804   Surety: Reuben Vaughan

BEAUFORD, Daniel   Sarah Hightower
    M.B. March 24, 1787   Surety: Thomas Jones

BEAVER, William   Elizabeth Hutcheson
    M.B. December 28, 1789   Surety: James Jones

BEDFORD, James   Frances Maynard
    M.B. November 14, 1786   Surety: William Maynard

BEDFORD, John   Mary Ann Marshall
    M.B. September 10, 1787   Francis Marshall
    Minister: John Williams
    Note: John Bedford of Charlotte County
    Note: John, son of Thomas (Sr.) and Mary Ligon
          (Coleman) Bedford

BELL, John   Mary Butler
    M.B. January 12, 1785   Surety: William Lucas

BENNETT, Anthony   Susanna Davis
    M.B. December 13, 1779   Surety: John Brown

BENNETT, Jonathon   Sarah Tanner
    M.B. December 17, 1793   Surety: Thomas Tanner

BENNETT, Jordan   Mary Ann Tanner
    M.B. March 14, 1791   M. March 17, 1791
    Minister: John King   Surety: Anthony Bennett

BENNETT, Jordan   Nancy Murfey
    M.B. December 15, 1795   M. December 17, 1795
    Minister: John Loyd   Surety: Thomas Tanner

BENNETT, Joseph   Nancy Lanier
    M.B. May 24, 1785   Surety: Ingram Vaughan

BENNETT, Joseph   Elizabeth Burrus
    M.B. April 9, 1787   Surety: Anthony Bennett

BENNETT, William   Tabitha Lanier
    M.B. October 1, 1807   Surety: Philip Roberts

BEVILL, Thomas   Nancy Keeton
    M.B. January 24, 1797   M. January 26, 1797
    Minister: William Creath   Surety: Hutchins Burton

BEVILL, William   Nancy Prewitt
    M.B. December 22, 1800   Surety: Thomas Johnson

BILBO, Allen Moss   Martha Farrar
    M.B. December 15, 1810   M. December 20, 1810
    Minister: James Meacham   Surety: Benjamin Whitlow

BILBO, John   Mary Clemonds
    M.B. September 28, 1786   Surety: Nicholas Bilbo

BILBO, John   Mary Nicholson
    M.B. April 2, 1807   Surety: George H. Baskervill

BILBO, Joseph   Jane Greer
    M.B. September 11, 1780   Surety: Zachariah Bevers
    Consent: Joseph Greer, father of Jane Greer

BINFORD, Thomas   Elizabeth Oslin
    M.B. December 25, 1786   Surety: John Oslin
    Consent: Jesse Oslin, father of Elizabeth

BINFORD, Thomas   Susanna Finch
    M.B. May 2, 1795   M. May 3, 1795
    Minister: John Loyd   Surety: William Finch

BINFORD, Thomas   Rebekah Thompson
    M.B. January 16, 1804   Surety: Edward Thompson

BING, James   Patsy Short
    M.B. January 8, 1789   Surety: Daniel Tucker
    Minister: Thomas Scott

BISHOP, Jeremiah   Elizabeth Colley
    M.B. February 8, 1802   Surety: Charles Colley
    Minister: William Creath

BLACK, Frederick   Elizabeth Lockett
    M.B. January 11, 1790   M. January 12, 1790
    Minister: John Williams   Surety: Royal Lockett
    Note: Frederick Black of Campbell County

BLACK, Stephen   Temperance Clay
    M.B. January 8, 1793   M. January 10, 1793
    Minister: John Williams   Surety: Britain Clay
    Consent: Charles and Pheby Clay parents
    Note: Stephen Black of Campbell County

BLACKBOURN, Clement   Mary Lewis
    M.B. October 21, 1784   Surety: Francis Lewis
    Note: Clement, son of Thomas Blackbourn
    Note: Clement moved to Madison County, Alabama

BLACKETTER, David   Mary F. Cox
    M.B. December 13, 1796   Surety: Edward Cox

BLACKETTER, William   Elizabeth Allgood
    M.B. December 24, 1793   Surety: Bartlett Cox

BLAKE, Benjamin   Sally Whobry
    M.B. April 3, 1809   M. April 6, 1809
    Minister: James Meacham   Surety: George B. Hamner

BLAND, John   Sally Burnett
    M.B. April 22, 1794   M. April 26, 1794
    Minister: Charles Ogburn   Surety: Anselm Bugg
    Consent: Elizabeth Burnett, mother of Sally

BLAND, Williamson   Dorcas Williams
    M.B. November 17, 1806   Surety: James Bugg
    Minister: James Meacham

BLANTON, Green   Nancy D. Overby
    M.B. February 15, 1810   M. February 22, 1810
    Minister: James Meacham   Surety: Adam Overby

BOOKER, Jonathon   Lucy Simmons
     M.B. August 10, 1795   Surety: Thomas Jones
     Minister: William Creath

BOOKER, Lowry   Phebe Cox
     M.B. December 11, 1780   Surety: John Clay
     Consent: John Cox, Senr., relation not stated

BOOKER, Reuben   Judy Bowen
     M.B. June 19, 1801   Surety: Daniel Tucker, Jr.

BOOKER, William   Martha Bozwell
     M.B. January 14, 1799   M. January 17, 1799
     Minister: William Creath   Surety: Benjamin Bozwell

BOOKER, William   Polly Finch
     M.B. November 10, 1802   Surety: John Puryear, Jr.
     Minister: William Richards

BOOTH, John   Sally Read Marshall
     M.B. April 9, 1805   Surety: John Johnson
     Consent: Richard Marshall, father of Sally

BOOTH, John   Elizabeth Mabry
     M.B. December 29, 1810   Surety: Edward Giles

BOSWELL, John   Mary Coleman
     M.B. February 16, 1784   Surety: James Coleman
     Consent: Cluverius Coleman, father of Mary
     Note: John Iveson Boswell, son of Joseph Boswell

BOSWELL, Joseph   Susanna Pettus
     M.B. December 9, 1805   M. December 24, 1805
     Minister: Thomas Hardie   Surety: Samuel Pettus, Sr.
     Note: Joseph, son of Ransom and Martha Boswell

BOTTOM, Anderson   Sally Hatchell
     M.B. May 30, 1809   M. May 31, 1809
     Minister: James Meacham   Surety: William H. Bugg

BOTTOM, Bolling   Martha Harper
     M.B. March 14, 1796   M. March 16, 1796
     Minister: John Neblett   Surety: Wyatt Harper
     Note: Bolling Bottom of Brunswick County

BOTTOM, Wilson   Elizabeth Richardson
     M.B. December 20, 1806   Surety: Nathaniel Moss
     Minister: James Meacham

BOWEN, Asa   Charlotte Bowen
     M.B. December 6, 1796   M. December 13, 1796
     Minister: John Loyd   Surety: Charles Bowen
     Note, Asa, son of Charles and Amey Bowen

BOWEN, Benjamin   Martha Sparks
    M.B. September 12, 1803   Surety: Zachariah Yancey

BOWEN, Charnel   Omea Bowen
    M.B. October 15, 1805   Surety: Berry Bowen

BOWEN, Elisha   * Magdala Salley
    M.B. August 24, 1803   Surety: John Turner, Jr.
    Minister: William Creath   * Magdelaine Salle'

BOWEN, Hughke *   Jincy Finn
    M.B. November 30, 1801   Surety: Littleberry Bowen
    * Hughberry Bowen
    Note: Brother of Littleberry Bowen

BOWEN, Jordan   Nancy Pearcy
    M.B. March 25, 1804   Surety: John Hudgins

BOWEN, Richard Jones   Betsy S. Kirks
    M.B. November 22, 1808   Surety: James Bowen

BOWEN, Zachariah   Mavel Drummond
    M.B. October 2, 1795   M. October 8, 1795
    Minister: Charles Ogburn   Surety: Thomas Drummond
    Note: Zachariah, son of James and Susannah Bowen

BOWERS, Sandefer   Elizabeth Vaughan
    M.B. December 14, 1790   Surety: Richard Edmondson

BOYD, Alexander   Matilda Burwell
    M.B. October 10, 1803   Surety: John Dortch
    Consent: Armistead Burwell, guardian for sister
    Minister: John Cameron
    Note: Matilda, daughter of Lewis Burwell, deceased

BOYD, Richard   Panthea Burwell
    M.B. November 19, 1799   Surety: John Wright
    Consent: Lewis Burwell, father of Panthea
    Minister: John Cameron

BOYD, Robert   Sarah Anderson Jones
    M.B. April 20, 1789   Surety: Major Butler
    Minister: Thomas Scott
    Consent: Alexander Boyd, father of Robert
    Consent: Tignal Jones, father of Sarah

BOYD, Robert   Tabitha Walker
    M.B. May 11, 1803   Surety: John Dortch
    Minister: John Cameron
    Note: Tabitha Walker, daughter of Henry and Martha
          Bolling Walker

BOYNTON, Elijah   Elizabeth Neal
    M.B. December 31, 1808   Surety: James Mealer

BRADLEY, John   Mary Taylor
    M.B. November 16, 1772   Surety: Lewis Speed

BRADLEY, Joseph   Rebecca Patillo
    M.B. February 17, 1794   M. February 27, 1794
    Minister: John Loyd   Surety: Solomon Patillo

BRAGG, David   Susanna Goodwin
    M.B. January 9, 1797   M. January 22, 1797
    Minister: John Loyd   Surety: Bennett Goodwin

BRAME, David   Barbara Hester
    M.B. November 28, 1807   M. December 3, 1807
    Minister: William Richards   Surety: James Hester

BRAME. Dickey   Anna Hutcheson
    M.B. January 29, 1795   M. February 5, 1795
    Minister: Charles Ogburn   Surety: Archibald Phillips
    Consent: Richard Hutcheson, Sr., father of Anna

BRAME, George W.   Dianna Clark
    M.B. April 9, 1804   M. April 17, 1804
    Minister: James Meacham   Surety: Lewis Roffe

BRAME, James C.   Elizabeth B. Daly
    M.B. September 9, 1806   M. September 11, 1806
    Minister: James Meacham   Surety: William Daly

BRAME, James D.   Susanna Brame
    M.B. October 23, 1810   M. November 1, 1810
    Minister: James Meacham   Surety: Warner L. Brame

BRAME, John   * Mary Norman
    M.B. March 18, 1768   Surety: John Norment
    * Probably Mary Norment

BRAME, John   Lilly Hester
    M.B. December 9, 1805   M. December 19, 1805
    Minister: William Richards
                        Surety: William W. V. Clausel

BRAME, Joseph   Jane Hester
    M.B. March 10, 1806   M. March 20, 1806
    Minister: William Richards
                        Surety: William W. V. Clausel

BRAME, Melchizedeck   Sarah Bailey
    M.B. February 1, 1797   M. February 2, 1797
    Minister: Samuel D. Brame   Surety: William Rowlett

BRAME, Samuel   Elizabeth Roffe
    M.B. September 21, 1802   Surety: Ingram Roffe
    Consent: James Brame, father of Samuel

BRAME, William   Hannah H. Clausel
    M.B. December 12, 1808   M. December 22, 1808
    Minister: William Richards
                        Surety: Alexander B. Puryear

BRANDON, Edward   Elizabeth Chavous
    M.B. March 10, 1806   Surety: Frederick Irby

BRESSIE, Francis   Sarah Royster
    M.B. April 13, 1778   Surety: Joseph Royster
    Note: Sarah, daughter of Joseph Royster
    Note: Francis, son of Francis and Elizabeth Bressie

BRIDGEWATER, William   Barbara Hester
    M.B. July 13, 1792   Surety: William Hundley
    Minister: James Read
    Note: Barbara, daughter of Abraham Hester, deceased

BRIGGS, James   Polly Arnold
    M.B. February 10, 1794   M. February 27, 1794
    Minister: Charles Ogburn   Surety: John Arnold
    Note: Polly, daughter of James and Mary Arnold

BRODIE, Dr. Edmond G.   Ann N. Haskins
    M.B. December 4, 1802   Surety: John S. Jeffries
    Consent: Christopher Haskins, father of Ann

BROGDON, William   Caty Carter
    M.B. August 31, 1786   Surety: Benjamin Ferrell

BROOKING, Robert Edward   Lucy Delony
    M.B. May 9, 1779   Surety: Henry Delony, Jr.
    Consent: Henry Delony, Sr., father of Lucy
    Consent: Vivian Brooking, father of Robert Edward
    Note: Robert E. Brooking of Amelia County

BROOKS, Robert Rose   Mary Parham
    M.B. November 20, 1780   Surety: Daniel Baugh
    Consent: Robert Brooks, father of Robert Rose who is
                under 21 years of age

BROOKS, Wade   Tabitha Jones
    M.B. January 7, 1796   M. January 9, 1796
    Minister: John Loyd   Surety: John Webb

                            20

BROWDER, Isham   Talitha Cox
    M.B. February 3, 1767   Surety: John Cox
    Consent: Mary Cox, mother and guardian of Talitha
    Consent: John Cox, brother of Talitha
    Note: Isham Browder of Halifax County

BROWDER, Thomas   Betsy Bland
    M.B. July 21, 1796   M. July 22, 1796
    Minister: William Creath   Surety: Jesse Bugg

BROWDER, William   Nancy Mitchell
    M.B. January 25, 1808   Surety: William Mitchell

BROWN, James   Sarah Hutson
    M.B. December 29, 1789   Surety: James Cox
    Minister: Thomas Scott

BROWN, Jeremiah   Elizabeth Douglas
    M.B. August 28, 1770   Surety: William Douglas

BROWN, Jeremiah   Mary Gregory
    M.B. November 10, 1806   Surety: Jesse Craddock

BROWN, Jesse   Ann Bolling Murray
    M.B. September 16, 1786   Surety: Samuel Goode
    Consent: Susanna Murray, mother of Ann
    Note: Ann Bolling, daughter of John Murray

BROWN, Jesse   Patsy Vaughan
    M.B. May 28, 1798   Surety: Thomas Vaughan

BROWN, John   Lucy Jeffries
    M.B. November 22, 1800   Surety; William Brown

BROWN, Pettus   Polly Cluverius Jeffries
    M.B. April 22, 1809   Surety: Thomas Brown
    Consent: Mercia Coleman, relation not stated

BROWN, Richard   Lucy Hester
    M.B. December 28, 1801   Surety: Littleberry Rudd
    Minister: William Richards   M. December 30, 1801

BROWN, William   Sally Hutcheson
    M.B. December 14, 1789   Surety: Richard Hutcheson
    Minister: Thomas Scott

BROWN, William   Mary C. Roffe
    M.B. March 10, 1806   M. March 13, 1806
    Minister: Charles Ogburn   Surety: Melchizedeck Roffe

BRUMMIT, Leroy   Jane Freeman
    M.B. December 7, 1800   Surety: Benjamin Freeman

BUGG, Benjamin   Anne Andrews
    M.B. September 3, 1785   Surety: Ephraim Andrews, Jr.
    Consent: Ephraim Andrews, Sr., father of Anne

BUGG, Benjamin   Tabitha Walden
    M.B. May 3, 1805   M. May 9, 1805
    Minister: James Meacham   Surety: James Noel

BUGG, Edmond   Sarah Jeffries
    M.B. December 10, 1792   M. December 13, 1792
    Minister: John Loyd   Surety: Swepson Jeffries

BUGG, Jacob   Sarah Davis
    M.B. July 27, 1791   Surety: Sherwood Bugg
    Consent: John Davis, father of Sarah

BUGG, Jacob   Mary Thweate Tucker
    M.B. September 11, 1798 Surety: Benjamin Tucker, Jr.

BUGG, James   Rebecca Pully
    M.B. December 8, 1800   M. December 11, 1800
    Minister: James Meacham   Surety: Samuel Bugg

BUGG, John   Rebeccah Mitchell
    M.B. December 17, 1788 Surety: James Sandifer, Jr.

BUGG, Samuel, Jr.   Elizabeth Bilbo
    M.B. March 25, 1794   Surety: Bennett Sandifer

BUGG, Sherwood   Sarah Speed
    M.B. December 31, 1787   Surety: Joseph Speed
    Minister: Thomas Scott

BUGG, William   Lucy Hix
    M.B. November 7, 1773   Surety: Amos Hix

BUGG, William   Fanny Holmes
    M.B. January 22, 1803   Surety: John Holmes

BUGG, Zachariah   Mary C. Taylor
    M.B. December 9, 1803   Surety: Roger Gregory

BULLINGTON, John   Bicy Reader
    M.B. March 20, 1797   M. March 23, 1797
    Minister: William Richards   Surety: John Cox
    Consent: Grace Reader, mother of Bicy

BULLOCK, William   Elizabeth Lewis
    M.B. August 20, 1766   Surety: Edmund Taylor
    Note: Elizabeth, widow of James Lewis, nee Elizabeth
        Taylor, sister of Edmund Taylor

BURNETT, Edmund   Rebecca Crowder
     M.B. October 31, 1797   M. November 20, 1797
     Minister: Charles Ogburn   Surety: Isaac Arnold
     Consent: John Crowder, father of Rebecca

BURNETT, Henry   Milly Crowder
     M.B. October 21, 1789   Surety: John Crowder

BURNETT, Matthew   Polly Thompson
     M.B. November 1, 1800   Surety: John Thompson
     Minister: William Creath

BURNETT, Phillip   Martha W. Andrews
     M.B. July 10, 1799   Surety: Isaac Arnold
     Consent: George Andrews, father of Martha
     Minister: Charles Ogburn

BURNETT, Robert   * Nancy Whoberry
     M.B. October 23, 1798   Surety: William Whoberry
     Consent: Jacob Whoberry, father of Nancy
     Note: Name later written by descendants as Hoobry *

BURNETT, Thomas   Elizabeth Jeffries
     M.B. August 4, 1785   Surety: George H. Baskervill
     Consent: Swepson Jeffries, Father of Elizabeth

BURNETT, William   Martha Jeffries
     M.B. October 1, 1794   M. October 2, 1794
     Minister: Charles Ogburn   Sur: Swepson Jeffries, Jr.
     Consent: Swepson Jeffries, Senr., father of Martha

BURNETT, William   Nancy Williams
     M.B. February 13, 1799   M: February 14, 1799
     Minister: Ebenezer Macgowan   Surety: Lewis Williams

BURRUS, George   Elizabeth Puryear
     M.B. October 8, 1804   Surety: Hutchins Burton
     Minister: John Adkinson

BURRUS, Wiley   Peggy Gordon
     M.B. August 14, 1809   M. August 30, 1809
     Minister: Matthew Dance   Surety: William Burton

BURTON, Allen   Rebeccah Hamblen
     M.B. March 22, 1786   Surety: Isaac Pully
     Note: Allen, son of Robert Burton

BURTON, Benjamin   Monica Humphries
     M.B. June 19, 1775   Surety: John Humphries

BURTON, Charles   Elizabeth Johnston
     M.B. September 9, 1793   Surety: Thomas Wilson

BURTON, Charles   Catherine Foster
     M.B. August 11, 1806   Surety: William Wills Green
     Note: William Wills Green, formerly of Amelia County

BURTON, Charles   Elizabeth Burrus
     M.B. November 9, 1807   Surety: Vinson Garner

BURTON, Elisha   Elizabeth Chamberlain
     M.B. January 14, 1805   Surety: Joseph B. Clausel
     Note: Elisha, son of Robert Burton

BURTON, James   Cuzzy Lambert
     M.B. December 8, 1792   M. December 13, 1792
     Minister: John Loyd   Surety: Mark Lambert Jackson

BURTON, John   Clary Vaughan
     M.B. February 20, 1787   Surety: Ambrose Vaughan
     Note: Ambrose Vaughan of Brunswick County

BURTON, John   Elizabeth R. Brame
     M.B. February 9, 1801   Surety: Edward Roffe
     Minister: William Creath
     Note: John, son of Robert Burton

BURTON, Micajah   Susanna Puryear
     M.B. July 3, 1791   M. July 18, 1791
     Minister: James Read   Surety: Robert Burton

BURTON, Owen   Mary Hester
     M.B. January 8, 1798   M. January 10, 1798
     Minister: William Richards Surety: Robert Marshall

BURTON, Robert   Milley Lambert
     M.B. July 9, 1800   Surety: James Burton
     Minister: Ebenezer Macgowan

BURTON, Thomas Hailey   Martha Humphries
     M.B. September 30, 1783   Surety: John Humphries

BURTON, William   Molly Brooks
     M.B. January 22, 1774   Surety: William Brooks

BURTON, William   Patsey Mitchell
     M.B. December 30, 1806   M. January 1, 1807
     Minister: James Meacham   Surety: Gideon Walker

BURTON, William   Jinney Carroll
     M.B. April 12, 1810   Surety: Jonas Burton

BURWELL, Armistead   Lucy Crawley
     M.B. November 14, 1791   Surety: Robert Crawley
     Note: Armistead, son of Lewis Burwell of "Stoneland"

BUTLER, John   Nancy Stone
    M.B. November 10, 1806   Surety: Edward Jones

BUTLER, John O.   Frances C. Hutcheson
    M.B. December 9, 1804   M. December 10, 1804
    Minister: James Meacham   Surety: William Browder

BUTLER, Joseph   Frances Oliver
    M.B. June 9, 1783   Surety: John Oliver

BUTLER, Lewis   Jincy J. Ryland
    M.B. January 2, 1805   Surety: Churchwell Curtis

BUTLER, Major   Elizabeth Oliver
    M.B. December 29, 1790   M. December 30, 1790
    Minister: Edward Almand   Surety: John Farrar

BYASEE, John   Milly Russell
    M.B. December 21, 1807   Surety: Theophilus Russell

CABINESS, Charles   Lucy Worsham Ingram
    M.B. January 5, 1795   M. January 8, 1795
    Minister: Charles Ogburn   Surety: William Burton
    Consent: Pines Ingram, father of Lucy

CABINESS, George   Jinny Elliott
    M.B. November 30, 1799   M. December 2, 1799
    Minister: William Richards   Surety: Thomas Finch
    Consent: Martin Elliott, father of Jinny

CALLIS, William   Frances Gregory
    M.B. December 13, 1790   M. December 22, 1790
    Minister: John Williams   Surety: Andrew Gregory

CALLOWAY, Achilles   Elizabeth Hudson
    M.B. February 9, 1795   Surety: Richard Hudson
    Minister: William Creath
    Note: Achilles Calloway from Pittsylvania County

CALLTHARP, John   Mary Crowder
    M.B. February 10, 1784   Surety: Samuel Edmundson

CAMP, George   Mary Palmer
    M.B. July 30, 1772   Surety: Nicholas Maynard

CAMP, John   Mary Smith, Widow
    M.B. May 12, 1783   Surety: George Tarry
    Note: Mary, widow of Drury Smith

CAMP, Richard   Nancy Hudson
    M.B. January 11, 1802   William Hudson
    Consent: John Hudson, father of Nancy
    Note: Richard Camp of Halifax County

CAMPBELL, Collin   Fanny Epperson
    M.B. November 30, 1785   Surety: John Campbell

CARDIN, Reuben   Stacy Bowen
    M.B. January 8, 1793   M. January 10, 1793
    Minister: William Creath   Surety: Zachariah Bowen
    Consent: John Cardin, father of Reuben
    Consent: James Bowen, father of Stacy

CARDIN, Robert   Lockey Hunt
    M.B. January 4, 1787   Surety: Joel Moore
    Consent: John Cardin, father of Robert
    Consent: William Hunt, father of Lockey

CARLETON, Gabriel   Elizabeth Edwards
    M.B. January 14, 1788   Surety: John Edwards
    Minister: Thomas Scott
    Note: Gabriel, son of Thomas Carleton

CARRIER, John   Elizabeth Parsons
    M.B. June 13, 1785   Surety: Francis Barnes
    Consent: Thomas Parsons, father of Elizabeth

CARROLL, Ezekiel   Martha Douglas
    M.B. April 13, 1805   Surety: Eli Elam

CARROLL, James   Sally Greffies
    M.B. December 12, 1786   Surety: Mark Lambert Jackson

CARROLL, John   Amey Crowder
    M.B. November 28, 1793   Surety: Daniel Tucker

CARROLL, John   Anne Crowder
    M.B. December 23, 1793   Surety: Richard Fox
    Minister: John Loyd   M. December 24, 1793

CARROLL, John   Caty Humphries
    M.B. April 22, 1797   Surety: William Carroll
    Minister: Charles Ogburn

CARROLL, William   Mary Crowder
    M.B. January 3, 1788   Surety: Bailey Turner

CARTER, Braxton   Polly Green
    M.B. June 9, 1802   Surety: Everard Green

CARTER, John   Polly Stevens
    M.B. December 12, 1788   Surety: Thomas Stevens

CARTER, Matthew   Sally Vowel
    M.B. August 13, 1804   Surety: William Birtchett

CARTER, Richard   Mary Haile
    M.B. January 14, 1793   Surety: Ellyson Crew

CARTER, Robert   Jinney Naish
    M.B. February 18, 1802   Surety: Abel Naish

CAVINESS, William   Elizabeth Culbreath
    M.B. February 8, 1796   Surety: Henry Hester

CAZY, William   Polly Evans
    M.B. December 23, 1786   Surety: Kinchen Chavous

CHAMBERS, Nathaniel   Mary Small
    M.B. September 6, 1790   Surety: James Chambers

CHAMBLISS, James   Mary Stigall
    M.B. November 10, 1785   Surety: Mial Wall

CHANDLER, Joel   Agness Light
    M.B. April 12, 1772   Surety: Nathaniel Hix

CHANDLER, Joel   Hannah Davis
    M.B. May 14, 1807   Surety: David Chandler
    Consent: Stephen P'Pool, guardian of Hannah

CHANDLER, Robert   Lucretia Graves
    M.B. February 28, 1797   Surety: John P, Finch
    Consents: Elijah and Lucretia Graves, parents of
              Lucretia   Minister: William Creath
    Note: Robert Chandler of Granville County, N. C.

CHANDLER, Samuel   Lina Stewart
    M.B. December 23, 1793   M. December 28, 1793
    Minister: William Creath   Surety: William Chandler

CHAVOUS, Allen   Sally Clanch
    M.B. September 7, 1804   Surety: Drury Johnson

CHAVOUS, Anthony   Rebecca Stewart
    M.B. September 10, 1792   Surety: Henry Royster
    Minister: James Read

CHAVOUS, Bolling   Sukey Thomason
    M.B. January 25, 1798   M. February 7, 1798
    Minister: Charles Ogburn   Surety: Banister Thomason
    Consent: Amy Thomason, mother of Susanna

CHAVOUS, Earby   Fanny McLin
    M.B. March 9, 1797   M. March 10, 1797
    Minister: John Loyd   Surety: Thomas McLin

CHAVOUS, Jacob   Pheby Scott
    M.B. December 8, 1800   M. December 24, 1800
    Minister: Edward Almand   Surety: Thomas A. Jones
    Consent: James Mayne, relation not stated

CHAVOUS, John   Sally Blair
    M.B. July 27, 1801   Surety: Thomas Cypress

CHAVOUS, Kinchen   Milly Chavous
    M.B. December 22, 1788   Surety: William Thomerson

CHAVOUS, William   Precilla Drew
    M.B. December 29, 1806   M. December 30, 1806
    Minister: William Richards   Surety: Benjamin Lewis

CHEATHAM, Daniel   Rebecca Cooper
    M.B. June 21, 1790   Surety: William Drumwright
    Consent: Elisha Arnold, guardian of Rebecca.
    Note: He states that Rebecca is the daughter of
          Francis Cooper, deceased

CHEATHAM, James   Ann Wilson
    M.B. February 9, 1784   Surety: John Wilson

CHEATHAM, James   Caty Johnson
    M.B. January 11, 1794   M. January 15, 1794
    Minister: John Neblett   Surety: Wyatt Harper

CHEATHAM, John   Nancy Vaughan
    M.B. February 23, 1808   Surety: Ambrose Vaughan

CHEATHAM, Obadiah   Lucy Jones
    M.B. December 21, 1787   Surety: William Drumwright
    Consent: Baalam Jones, father of Lucy

CHEATHAM, Samuel   Elizabeth Keeton
    M.B. May 12, 1800   M. May 15, 1800
    Minister: Matthew Dance   Surety: Warner Keeton

CHEATHAM, Samuel   Nancy Davis
    M.B. December 22, 1803   Surety: William Davis

CHRISTOPHER, Jacobus   Lurita Dennis
    M.B. _____ *   Moses Overton
    Note: Jacobus, son of David Christopher
    * Date not stated in bond, but probably after 1784
      for Jacobus under age in will of David Christopher

28

CHURCH, Robert   Elizabeth Jones
    M.B. December 9, 1799   Surety: Richard Jones

CIRKES, Jesse *   Ellender Ornsby
    M.B. May 11, 1786   Surety: William Singleton
    * Probably Jesse Kirks

CLACK, John S.   Ann E. Walker
    M.B. September 13, 1790   Surety: Henry Walker
    Note: Ann, daughter of Henry and Martha Bolling
        Walker

CLARDY, James   Luritta Daniel
    M.B. June 18, 1810   Surety: William Daniel

CLARK, Archibald   Sarah Northington
    M.B. June 24, 1807   Surety: Scarborough Penticost
    Consent: Nathan Northington, father of Sarah

CLARK, Elisha   Nancy Waller
    M.B. January 2, 1810   Surety: John Waller

CLARK, Henry   Elizabeth Wilson
    M.B. January 6, 1801   Surety: Henry Wilson

CLARK, James   Nancy Williamson
    M.B. December 10, 1792   M. December 20, 1792
    Minister: James Read   Surety: John Williamson

CLARK, Jesse   Martha Jones
    M.B. October 23, 1799   Surety: James Jones
    Minister: William Creath

CLARK, Joseph   Sally Mullins
    M.B. February 9, 1795   M. February 24, 1795
    Minister: William Richards   Surety: James Hudson

CLARK, Richard   Caty Wall
    M.B. January 20, 1800   Surety: Richard Overby

CLARK, William   Jinny Insco
    M.B. September 3, 1785   Surety: James Insco
    Consent: John Clark, father of William

CLARKE, Carter   Martha Farrar
    M.B. November 9, 1778   Surety: Edward Finch
    Consent: John Farrar, relation not stated
    Note: He states that Patty Farrar is 21 years old

CLARKE, Joseph   Sarah Toone
    M.B. December 14, 1795   Surety: Bolling Clarke

CLAUNCH, Dennis   Nancy Beasley
    M.B. November 8, 1803   Surety: Willima Justice

CLAUNCH, Jeremiah   Prudence Jackson
    M.B. March 21, 1799   Surety: Samuel Allgood

CLAUNCH, Matthew   Elizabeth Allgood
    M.B. August 29, 1799   Surety: Samual Allgood

CLAUNCH, William   Betsy Alvis
    M.B. August 5, 1793   Surety: William Blacketter
    Consent: Jeremiah Claunch, father of William
    Consent: David Alvis, father of Betsy

CLAUSEL, Joseph B.   Susannah Brame
    M.B. February 23, 1799   M. February 28, 1799
    Minister: William Richards Surety: John Puryear, Jr.

CLAUSEL, William W. Va.   Elizabeth Brame
    M.B. July 19, 1803   M. July 21, 1803
    Minister: William Richards Surety: John Puryear, Jr.

CLAY, Eleazar   Elizabeth Whitehead
    M.B. January 7, 1789   Surety: Richard Whitehead
    Note: Eleazar Clay of Chesterfield County

CLAY, John   Sally Coleman
    M.B. February 11, 1805   Surety: James Coleman
    Minister: William Richards M. February 16, 1805

CLAY, Tolbert   Nanny Harris
    M.B. April 7, 1805   Surety: John E. Harris

CLEATON, Isham   Lucy Taylor
    M.B. March 8, 1809   Surety: William Cleaton

CLEATON, John   Martha Taylor
    M.B. November 10, 1787   Surety: David Taylor

CLEATON, Thomas   Nancy Webb
    M.B. November 27, 1787   Surety: Abel Dortch

CLEATON, Thomas, Senr.   Lucy Malone
    M.B. March 3, 1808   Surety: Thomas Nance
    Minister: James Meacham

CLEATON, Woodley   Sally Harris
    M.B. January 2, 1805   Surety: John Harris

CLAIBORNE, Leonard (Cliborne)   Mary M. Stokes
    M.B. May 13, 1799   Surety: John Powell

CLEMENTS, Austin   Mary M. Mayne
    M.B. February 11, 1805   M. February 14, 1805
    Minister: Edward Almand   Surety: Henry W. Overby
    Consent: James Mayne, father of Mary
    Note: Austin Clements of Charlotte County

CLEMENTS, William   Sarah Bignal
    M.B. June 5, 1789   Surety: Joseph Speed
    Minister: Thomas Scott

CLEMMONDS, Edmund   Sarah L. Wright
    M.B. November 12, 1805   Surety: Richard Moss

CLEMMONDS, Matthew   Elizabeth Allgood
    M.B. March 3, 1789   Surety: John Allgood

COBBS, Thomas   Elizabeth H. Phillips
    M.B. October 23, 1806   M. October 24, 1806
    Minister: Charles Ogburn   Surety: John Dortch

COCKE, James   Elizabeth Moss
    M.B. July 26, 1800   Surety: Lewis Moss

COLE, Bartlett   Levina Tisdale
    M.B. October 27, 1789   Surety: Edward Tisdale
    Minister: Thomas Scott

COLE, James   Micah Bevill
    M.B. March 13, 1797   Surety: Francis M. Neal
    Minister: William Creath

COLE, Robert   Mary Stewart
    M.B. December 31, 1802   M. January 2, 1803
    Minister: William Creath   Surety: Martin Cousins

COLE, Thomas   Anne Kirkland
    M.B. December 21, 1792   M. December 24, 1792
    Minister: William Creath   Surety: James Cole

COLEMAN, Burwell   Martha Daws
    M.B. January 28, 1794   M. February 1, 1794
    Minister: William Creath   Surety: Isaac Daws

COLEMAN, Cain   Betsy Grigg
    M.B. April 11, 1791   Surety: Jesse Grigg

COLEMAN, Cain   Sally Inge
    M.B. January 5, 1803   Surety: Richard Taylor

COLEMAN, Cain   Anne Reamey
    M.B. January 9, 1804   Surety: Richard Carter

31

```
COLEMAN, Daniel                              Elizabeth Haskins
    M.B. November 14, 1791           Surety:  Henry Towns
    Consent: Thomas Haskins, father of Elizabeth
    Note: Henry Towns of Halifax County
    Note: Daniel Coleman of Pittsylvania County

COLEMAN, Daniel                                Susanna Overton
    M.B. September 14, 1801          Surety: John Overton
    Minister: William Creath

COLEMAN, James                                  Sarah Whitehead
    M.B. November 14, 1785           Surety: Richard Swepson
    Note: James, son of Cluverius Coleman

COLEMAN, John                                    Martha Pettus
    M.B. December 11, 1799           Surety: William Stone
    Minister: William Creath
    Note: John, son of Cluverius Coleman

COLEMAN, Roderick                                   Lucy Daws
    M.B. December 18, 1794            M. December 25, 1794
    Minister: Charles Ogburn             Surety: Isaac Daws
    Consent: James Daws, father of Lucy

COLEMAN, Thomas                                 Sally Rowlett
    M.B. January 5, 1799             M. January 10, 1799
    Minister: William Creath         Surety: William Brown
    Consent: William Rowlett, father of Sally
    Note: Thomas, son of Cluverius Coleman

COLEMAN, William B.                            Matilda Baptist
    M.B. June 2, 1803            Surety: Joseph N. Meredith
    Minister: William Richards
    Consent: William Glanville Baptist, father of Matilda
    Note: William B. Coleman, of Spottsylvania County

COLES, Tucker                                   Helen Skipwith
    M.B. May 21, 1810           Surety: John S. Ravenscroft
    Minister: George Micklejohn
    Consent: Jean Skipwith, mother of Helen
    Note: Tucker Coles of Albemarle County

COLEY, David                                 Elizabeth Matthews
    M.B. March 12, 1787         Surety: William Wills Green

COLEY, Isham                                    Frances Weekes
    M.B. April 9, 1787              Surety: George Tucker

COLEY, Thomas                                 Catherine Tucker
    M.B. February 24, 1800         Surety: Leonard Keeton

COLLEY, Samuel                               Obedience Williams
    M.B. March 24, 1785            Surety: Thomas Clark
```

COLLIER, Frederick   Ann Lark
    M.B. September 4, 1781   Surety: Edward Pennington

COLLIER, Howell   Hannah Creedle
    M.B. November 16, 1793   Surety: Lewis Collier

CONNAWAY, John   Susanna Royster
    M.B. November 19, 1810   M. November 24, 1810
    Minister: William Richards
                            Surety: Alexander B. Puryear

CONNELL, Benjamin   Martha Hatch
    M.B. August 27, 1788   Surety: William Taylor
    Consent: Freeman Short, guardian and father-in-law of
            Martha Hatch
    Note: Benjamin, son of Daniel Connell

CONNELL, James   Jane Pennington
    M.B. August 8, 1785   Surety: John Adams

CONNER, William   Martha Carroll
    M.B. September 18, 1804   Surety: Dennis Roberts

COOK, Herbert   Penelope Taylor
    M.B. December 20, 1802   Surety: John Taylor

COOK, Herbert   Sally Walker
    M.B. November 6, 1805   Surety: Tilman Elder

COOK, Kirby   Lizzy Adams
    M.B. January 2, 1788   Surety: Thomas Adams
    Note: Lizzy, daughter of Thomas and Lucy Adams

COOK, William   Fanny Rainey
    M.B. May 5, 1803   Surety: Buckner Rainey

COOPER, Francis   Betty Arnold
    M.B. April 25, 1769   Surety: James Arnold
    Note: Francis Cooper of Amelia County
    Note: Betty, daughter of James (Sr.) and Martha
            Arnold

COUCH, John   Susanna Smith
    M.B. October 25, 1799   Surety: Archer Smith
    Note: Susanna, daughter of John and Martha Smith

COUCH, Thomas   Sarah Gregory
    M.B. November 26, 1801   Surety: Archibald Smith
    Minister: William Richards

COUSINS, Austin   Elizabeth Brandon
    M.B. _____, 1802 *   Surety: Robert Cole
    * Bond torn, date illegible

COUSINS, Martin   Jincy Cole
    M.B. December 31, 1802   Surety: Robert Cole
    Minister: William Creath

COUZENS, Peter   Phibby A. Marshall
    M.B. December 15, 1800   M. December 24, 1800
    Minister: William Richards   Surety: Francis Marshall

COX, Archer   Polly Lewis Hatsel
    M.B. February 8, 1802   Surety: John Talley

COX, Banister   Rebecca Burrus
    M.B. October 26, 1803   Surety: John Pritchett
    Minister: William Creath

COX, Bartley   Susanna Carleton
    M.B. November 12, 1781   Surety: Asa Oliver
    Note: Susanna, daughter of Thomas Carleton

COX, Bartley   Lucy Allgood
    M.B. September 18, 1786   M. September 20, 1786
    Minister: John Marshall   Surety: Allen Burton

COX, Edward   Dianna Holloway
    M.B. December 31, 1767   Surety: Henry Delony

COX, Edward   Sally Brown
    M.B. January 3, 1795   Surety: Joseph Hamilton

COX, John, Jr.   Martha B. Hall
    M.B. July 11, 1803   M. July 14, 1803
    Minister: William Richards   Surety: William Marshall

COX, Kennon   Pricilla Smith
    M.B. March 14, 1803   Surety: John Morgan
    Minister: William Creath

COX, Samuel   Sally Hutt
    M.B. July 16, 1806   M. July 17, 1806
    Minister: James Meacham   Surety: Archer Cox

COX, Thomas   Margary Hudson
    M.B. March 17, 1794   M. March 18, 1794
    Minister: William Creath   Surety: David Hudson

COX, Thomas   Mary Draper
    M.B. March 7, 1796   M. March 8, 1796
    Minister: William Creath   Surety: Thomas Pritchett

CRADDOCK, David   Nancy Neal
    M.B. October 25, 1800   Surety: G. H. Baskervill

34

CRAIG, Rev. James   Mary Tarry, Spinster
    M.B. February 19, 1766   Surety: Edmund Taylor
    Note: Rev. James Craig of Lunenburg County
    Note: Mary, daughter of Samuel Tarry

CREATH, William   Lucy Brame
    M.B. June 11, 1792   M. June 14, 1792
    Minister: John Williams   Surety: Reuben Vaughan
    Consent: Elizabeth Brame, mother of Lucy
    Note: Lucy Brame, orphan of Thomas Brame

CREEDLE, Drury   Patsy Mason
    M.B. September 22, 1798   M. September 25, 1798
    Minister: Charles Ogburn   Surety: Jeremiah Adams

CREEDLE, Edmond   Mary Ann Talley
    M.B. February 11, 1791   Surety: Drury Creedle

CRENSHAW, John   Elizabeth Walker
    M.B. December 14, 1801   Surety: Thomas A. Jones

CREW, Charles   Nancy Hutt
    M.B. January 11, 1808   Surety: Samuel Cox

CREW, Ellyson   Sally Carter
    M.B. June 4, 1790   Surety: Winkfield Hayes
    Minister: James Read

CREWS, John   Sarah Nash
    M.B. July 25, 1782   Surety: Nathaniel Moss

CROOK, William   Martha Edwards
    M.B. April 11, 1791   M. April 13, 1791
    Minister: Edward Almand   Surety: John Edwards, Jr.

CROW, John   Martha Easter
    M.B. December 28, 1802   Surety: Jeremiah Adams

CROW, William   Nancy Thompson
    M.B. December 3, 1799   Surety: Charles Thompson
    Minister: Charles Ogburn
    Consent: John Crow, father of William

CROWDER, Abraham   Martha Loyd
    M.B. December 7, 1805   Surety: Elijah Crowder

CROWDER, Anderson   Polly Brummell
    M.B. January 20, 1796   M. January 28, 1796
    Minister: William Richards Surety: Abram Crowder, Jr.

CROWDER, David   Easter Jones
    M.B. April 30, 1795   Surety: Charles Kelly

CROWDER, Elijah   Rebekah Lloyd
    M.B. August 9, 1803   Surety: Richard Crowder, Sr.

CROWDER, Frederick I.   Milly Bowen
    M.B. December 4, 1797   Surety: James Bowen
    Minister: Charles Ogburn

CROWDER, Gardiner   Amy Tucker
    M.B. December 4, 1788   Surety: David Crowder

CROWDER, George   Nancy Bailey
    M.B. January 26, 1798   Surety: Richard Crowder
    Minister: William Creath

CROWDER, George   Sally Wright
    M.B. October 28, 1803   Surety: Elijah Crowder

CROWDER, James   Betsy Minor
    M.B. December 28, 1795   M. December 31, 1795
    Minister: William Creath   Surety: George Minor

CROWDER, James   Elizabeth Tucker
    M.B. December 12, 1810   Surety: Daniel Tucker, Sr.

CROWDER, Larkin   Lucy Rottenberry
    M.B. September 29, 1789   Surety: Samuel Rottenberry

CROWDER, Miles T.   Susannah B. Jeffries
    M.B. October 27, 1806   M. November 5, 1806
    Minister: James Meacham   Surety: Achilles Jeffries

CROWDER, Nathaniel   Martha Rainey
    M.B. November 25, 1805   Surety: Buckner Rainey

CROWDER, Richard   Lucy Clausel
    M.B. February 13, 1797   Surety: Richard Hutcheson
    Minister: William Creath

CROWDER, Robert   Lively Hasten
    M.B. September 2, 1788   M. September 11, 1788
    Minister: Edward Almand   Surety: Absolem Hasten

CROWDER, Thomas   Fanny Rhodes
    M.B. March 29, 1785   Surety: John Rhodes

CROWDER, Thomas   Elizabeth Puryear
    M.B. February 14, 1786   Surety: Solomon Draper
    Minister: John Marshall

CROWDER, Thomas   Patsy Russell
    M.B. December 18, 1787   M. January 14, 1788
    Minister: Edward Almand   Surety: Thomas Jones
    Consent: Ann Russell, mother of Patsy

CRUTCHFIELD, Adams   Nancy House
    M.B. January 3, 1810   Surety: Bartley Cheatham

CRUTCHFIELD, Samuel   Patsy Ellis
    M.B. December 25, 1804   Surety: Jesse Perkinson

CULBREATH, James   Polly Monroe
    M.B. December 12, 1803   Surety: Ellyson Crew

CULBREATH, John   Mary Clark
    M.B. December 13, 1790   Surety: Elijah Graves

CULBREATH, Thomas   Polly Culbreath
    M.B. May 8, 1809   Surety: Hughes Matthews

CULBREATH, William   Tempe Wiles
    M.B. March 13, 1804   Surety: Isaac Pinson

CUNNINGHAM, James   Alice Marshall
    M.B. July 10, 1809   M. July 22, 1809
    Minister: William Richards   Surety: Robert Marshall

CUNNINGHAM, William   Sally Marshall
    M.B. December 10, 1798   M. December 20, 1798
    Minister: William Richards   Surety: Robert Marshall

CURTIS, Churchwell   Rebecca Johnson
    M.B. June 17, 1801   Surety: Jesse Curtis

CURTIS, Elemeleck   Polly Nunnelly
    M.B. January 2, 1798   Surety: Micajah Gwaltney
    Minister: Charles Ogburn

CURTIS, Elie   Nancy Drummond
    M.B. January 28, 1794   M. January 31, 1794
    Minister: Charles Ogburn   Surety: Thomas Drummond
    Consent: Jane Drummond, mother of Nancy

CURTIS, Jesse   Mary Moore
    M.B. February 27, 1792   James Moore

CURTIS, John   Betsy Johnson
    M.B. December 19, 1806   M. December 21, 1806
    Minister: Charles Ogburn   Surety: Crafford McDaniel

CURTIS, Zachariah   Sally Powers
    M.B. February 16, 1795   Surety: Drury Creedle
    Minister: Charles Ogburn

37

CUTTS, William   Mary Mullins
    M.B. November 22, 1791   M. December 25, 1791
    Minister: John Williams   Surety: John Ragsdale

DACUS, Alexander   Jane Duprey
    M.B. November 17, 1789   Surety: Drury Duprey
    Note: Alexander Dacus of Lunenburg County

DALEY, Ambrose   Sarah Taylor
    M.B. January 30, 1809   Surety: James Taylor

DALY, Daniel   Elizabeth Holmes
    M.B. December 22, 1788   Surety: Sherwood Smith

DALEY, Daniel   Elizabeth Bugg
    M.B. July 1, 1794   M. July 3, 1794
    Minister: John Loyd   Surety: Abel Dortch

DALY, Josiah   Jinny McKinney
    M.B. October 21, 1795   Surety: Bennett Goodwin
    Minister: John Loyd
    Note: Josiah, son of John Daly *
    Note: Name Daly spelled variously as Daley, Dailey

DALY, Josiah, Jr.   Mary Moody
    M.B. November 14, 1800   Surety: John Daly, Jr.

DALY, John   Mary Russell
    M.B. March 11, 1782   Surety: Samuel Goode

DALEY, Vines   Rebecca Adams
    M.B. October 14, 1795   Surety: William Adams
    Minister: John Loyd   M: October 15, 1795

DALY, William   Lucy Abernathy
    M.B. March 10, 1807   M. March 12, 1807
    Minister: Charles Ogburn
                              Surety: Tignal Abernathy, Jr.
    Consent: Burwell Abernathy, father of Lucy

DANCE, Stephen   Elizabeth Briggs
    M.B. May 11, 1805   Surety: Charles Ogburn

DANIEL, Martin   Polly Daniel
    M.B. June 9, 1800   Surety: Thomas Daniel

DANIEL, Samuel   Martha Short
    M.B. November 13, 1809   M. November 16, 1809
    Minister: James Meacham   Surety: Henry Wall

DANIEL, Starky   Frances Royster
    M.B. January 4, 1803   M. January 5, 1803
    Minister: Baalam Ezell   Surety: Robert Shanks

DANIEL, Walter   Jane Puryear
    M.B. May 2, 1804   Surety: Benjamin Bugg
    Consent: Peter Bailey - Relation not stated

DANIEL, William   Elizabeth Wootton
    M.B. January 9, 1806   Surety: John Winckler

DANIEL, William   Elizabeth Short
    M.B. June 29, 1807   Surety: Wyatt Short

DAVIS, Charles   Elizabeth Hopkins
    M.B. December 11, 1784   Surety: John Hopkins

DAVIS, Hardaway   Elizabeth Davis
    M.B. August 12, 1771   Surety: Capt. William Davis

DAVIS, James   Sarah Holmes
    M.B. March 9, 1767   Surety: John Ballard, Jr.
    Note: Sarah, daughter of Isaac Holmes

DAVIS, John   Rebecca Watson
    M.B. November 11, 1778   Surety: Michael Watson

DAVIS, John   Phebey Floyd
    M.B. November 12, 1787   Surety: Charles Floyd

DAVIS, John, Jr.   Susanna Swepson
    M.B. March 28, 1786   Surety: Richard Swepson
    Minister: John Cameron

DAVIS, John, Jr.   Rebecca Ballard
    M.B. December 10, 1804   Surety: John Holmes, Jr.

DAVIS, Joshua   Nancy Wright
    M.B. January 3, 1805   Surety: William Wright

DAVIS, Matthew H.   Polly Lett
    M.B. December 22, 1801   Surety: Hardaway Lett
    Consent: Joseph Lett, Senr., father of Polly

DAVIS, William   Martha Thompson
    M.B. September 17, 1765   Surety: Wells Thompson
    Note: William Davis of Brunswick County

DAVIS, William   Mary Cheatham
    M.B. October 10, 1804   Surety: Daniel Cheatham
    Minister: William Creath

DAWS, James   Elizabeth T. Ferrell
    M.B. June 11, 1798   M. July 19, 1798
    Minister: William Creath   Surety: Hubbard Ferrell

DECKER, Henry   Patsy Talley
    M.B. December 30, 1791   Surety: William Decker

DEDMAN, Henry   Jincy White
    M.B. May 11, 1795   M. May 18, 1795
    Minister: William Richards   Surety: William White

DEDMAN, John   Elizabeth White
    M.B. February 11, 1799   M. February 12, 1799
    Minister: William Richards   Surety: Henry H. Dedman

DeGraffenreid, Francis   Ermin Boswell
    M.B. November 12, 1781   Surety: Asa Oliver
    Consent: Joseph Boswell, father of Ermin

DELONY, Edward   Elizabeth W. Lucas
    M.B. November 28, 1796   M. December 1, 1796
    Minister: John Loyd   Surety: William Delony
    Consent: William Lucas, father of Elizabeth

DENNIS, Matthew   Nancy Griffin
    M.B. May 8, 1797   Surety: Jacobus Christopher

DICKINS, Samuel   Jane Vaughan
    M.B. May 25, 1801   Surety: John Wilson

DIXON, Benjamin   Elizabeth Wagstaff
    M.B. November 20, 1800   M. December 9, 1800
    Minister: William Richards   Surety: John Wagstaff

DORTCH, Abel   Sally Taylor
    M.B. May 24, 1785   Surety: Goodwyn Taylor

DORTCH, Abel   Mary Holmes
    M.B. October 29, 1793   M. October 31, 1793
    Minister: John Loyd   Surety: David Dortch

DORTCH, David   Betsy Taylor
    M.B. May 30, 1798   M. May 31, 1798
    Minister: Ebenezer Macgowan   Surety: Abel Dortch

DORTCH, Jesse   Ora Saunders
    M.B. January 24, 1792   M. January 26, 1792
    Minister: John Loyd   Surety: Jacob Bugg
    Consent: Mary Saunders, mother of Ora

DORTCH, Lewis   Mary Speed
    M.B. January 2, 1796   M. January 9, 1796
    Minister: John Loyd   Surety: James Speed

DORTCH, Newman   Sarah Speed
    M.B. March 29, 1800   M. March 30, 1800
    Minister: Ebenezer Macgowan   Surety: John Dortch

DORTCH, Noah   Ann Lucas
    M.B. April 25, 1780   Surety: William Baskervill
    Note: Noah Dortch, Deputy Clerk of Mecklenburg County

DORTCH, William   Susanna Burton
    M.B. September 29, 1786   Surety: Robert Pennington

DOUGLAS, David   Martha Jones
    M.B. November 6, 1777   Surety: Francis Lightfoot

DOUGLAS, James   Nancy Johnson
    M.B. October 21, 1808   Surety: Terasha Johnson

DRUMMOND, David   Nancy Johnson
    M.B. November 27, 1787   Surety: Howell Johnson
    Consent: James Johnson - Relation not stated

DRUMWRIGHT, Ephraim   Elizabeth Pennington
    M.B. _____ 3, 1808 *   Surety: Wyatt Harper
    * Month not stated in bond

DRUMWRIGHT, James   Lytha Crowder
    M.B. October 9, 1794   M. October 23, 1794
    Minister: John Loyd   Surety: William Drumwright
    Consent: Richard Crowder, father of Lytha

DRUMWRIGHT, Thomas   Sarah Oslin Williams
    M.B. January 18, 1804   Surety: Lewis Williams
    Note: Sarah, daughter of Lewis Williams, Sr.

DRUMWRIGHT, William, Jr.   Libelar Crowder
    M.B. July 14, 1797   M. July 21, 1797
    Minister: Charles Ogburn   Surety: William Drumwright

DRUMWRIGHT, William, Jr.   Lucy Gee
    M.B. February 28, 1803   Surety: Thomas Drumwright
    Consent: Jones Gee, father of Lucy

DUGGER, William   Jean Stainback
    M.B. October 23, 1804   Surety: James Stainback
    Minister: William Creath
    Note: William Dugger of Brunswick County

DUNNINGTON, Reuben   Polly Wright
    M.B. July 11, 1798   Surety: William Wright
    Consent: Reuben Wright, father of Polly

DUNSTON, Miles   Nancy Stewart
    M.B. February 18, 1802   Surety: Thomas Spence

DUPREE, John   Nancy Short
    M.B. December 11, 1787   Surety: Thomas Buford
    Consent: Jacob and Mary Short, parents of Nancy
    Note: John Dupree of Brunswick County

DUPREY, Drury   Ann Atkinson
    M.B. March 8, 1784   Surety: John Crews
    Consent: Median Atkinson, mother of Ann
    Note: Median Atkinson, widow, married Lewis Duprey

DUPREY, Lewis   Median Atkinson
    M.B. October 11, 1784   Consent Drury Duprey
    Minister: Henry Lester

DUTY, Benjamin   Mary Wagstaff
    M.B. November 20, 1804   Surety: Bazzell Wagstaff
    Minister: William Richards
    Consent: John Wagstaff, father of Mary

EARLES, Presley   Elizabeth Pointer
    M.B. May 13, 1807   Surety: Roberts Nanney

EDMUNDS, Abel   Dolly Hudgins
    M.B. February 24, 1800   Surety: James Hudgins

EDMONDSON, John   Judith Clay
    M.B. October 6, 1792   Surety: Coleman Edmondson

EDMONDSON, Robert Spilsby   Nancy Singleton
    M.B. January 29, 1803   Surety: Thomas Crow
    Consent: Patsy Singleton, mother of Nancy

EDMONDSON, Thomas   Milly Arnold
    M.B. August 8, 1796   M. August 11, 1796
    Minister: Charles Ogburn   Surety: Jeremiah Arnold
    Note: Milly, daughter of James (Jr) and Mary Arnold

EDMUNDSON, Banister   Janey Davis
    M.B. December 16, 1793   M. December 19, 1793
    Minister: William Creath   Surety: George B. Hamner
    Consent: John Davis, father of Janey

EDMUNDSON, Benjamin   Keziah Hood
    M.B. October 17, 1785   Surety: Charles Hood

EDWARDS, George R.   Catherine Simmons
    M.B. January 12, 1797   Surety: Joseph Simmons

EDWARDS, John   Sarah Hyde
    M.B. November 8, 1784   Surety: Burwell Russell

EDWARDS, Thomas   Agness Hobson
    M.B. November 6, 1798   M. November 7, 1798
    Minister: William Creath   Surety: Charles Patterson

EDWARDS, Thomas   Caty Wall
    M.B. March 10, 1800   Surety: Thomas Daniel

EDWARDS, William   Sarah Kirkland
    M.B. February 13, 1798   Surety: Jeffrey Mustian
    Minister: Charles Ogburn

ELAM, Alexander   * Janey Norment
    M.B. March 14, 1785   March 17, 1785
    Minister: John Williams   Surety: Thomas Norment
    * Minister's return says Jane Norman

ELAM, Edward   Martha Smith
    M.B. November 13, 1786   Surety: Edward Finch
    Consent: John Smith, father of Martha

ELAM, John   Polly W. Garner
    M.B. October 23, 1797   M. October 26, 1797
    Minister: William Richards   Surety: Archibald Clark
    Consent: James Garner, father of Polly

ELAM, John   Elizabeth Elam
    M.B. October 13, 1806   M. October 23, 1806
    Minister: William Richards   Surety: James Hurt

ELAM, Peter   Susanna Gregory
    M.B. August 8, 1791   M. August 18, 1791
    Minister: John Loyd   Surety: Andrew Gregory

ELAM, Samuel   Martha Garner
    M.B. October 13, 1800   M. November 6, 1800
    Minister: Edward Almand   Surety: John Elam
    Consent: James Garner, father of Martha

ELAM, William   Patience Hurt
    M.B. November 19, 1810   M. December 12, 1810
    Minister: William Richards   Surety: William Hurt

ELDER, Tilman
    M.B. December 17, 1798
    Minister: John Neblett
                        Elizabeth Walker
                        M. December 24, 1798
                        Surety: John Holloway

ELDER, Tilman — M.B. December 17, 1798 — Minister: John Neblett — Elizabeth Walker — M. December 24, 1798 — Surety: John Holloway

ELIBECK, John D.
    M.B. July 18, 1808
    Elizabeth Hutcheson
    Surety: John Hutcheson

ELLINGTON, David
    M.B. December 2, 1793
    Minister: John Williams
    Letitia Cox
    M. December 19, 1793
    Surety: Thomas Green

ELLINGTON, William
    M.B. December 17, 1807
    Leannah Johnson
    Surety: John Johnson

ELLIOTT, William
    M.B. December 20, 1809
    Rebecca Boothe
    Surety: Reuben Boothe

EPPERSON, Joseph
    M.B. October 10, 1803
    Polly Hundley
    Surety: William Hundley

EUBANK, James
    M.B. December 1, 1801
    Susanna Dailey
    Surety: John Ferguson

EUBANK, William
    M.B. January 15, 1800
    Minister: Charles Ogburn
    Mary A. Holmes
    M. January 16, 1800
    Surety: Pennington Holmes

EVANS, Charles
    M.B. August 17, 1796
    Minister: John Loyd
    Martha Jeffries
    M. August 18, 1796
    Surety: Kenchen Chavous

EVANS, Evan
    M.B. December 24, 1807
    Polly Lunsford
    Surety: John Wright

EVANS, Isaac
    M.B. December 24, 1792
    Minister: William Creath
    Dicey Stewart
    M. December 25, 1792
    Surety: William Baskervill

EVANS, John
    M.B. November 5, 1792
    Temperance Clay
    Surety: John F. Reazon

EVANS, John
    M.B. September 11, 1800
    Betsy Massey
    Surety: Stephen Evans

EVANS, Ludwell
    M.B. February 25, 1783
    Consent: Edward Hogan, father of Mary
    Mary Hogan
    Surety: Edward Finch

EVANS, Ludwell
    M.B. November 19, 1810
    Minister: William Richards
    Jane B. Hardy
    M. December 20, 1810
    Surety: John S. Jeffries

EVANS, Matthew   Becky Barnett
    M.B. October 5, 1804   Surety: John Barnett

EVANS, Peter   Elizabeth Ornsby
    M.B. September 1, 1792   M. September 4, 1792
    Minister: John Loyd   Surety: Jeremiah Singleton

EVANS, Robin   Amy Stewart
    M.B. February 13, 1809   M. February 17, 1809
    Minister: William Richards   Surety: James Chavous

EVANS, Starling   Letty Thompson
    M.B. October 12, 1801   M. October 15, 1801
    Minister: William Richards   Surety: Bernard Thompson

EVANS, Stephen   Milly Mason
    M.B. November 22, 1797   M. November 23, 1797
    Minister: Charles Ogburn   Surety: Ananias Grainger

EVANS, William   Ede Hogan
    M.B. April 10, 1775   Surety: Edward Hogan

EVANS, William   Polly Walker
    M.B. December 8, 1802   M. December 9, 1802
    Minister: James Meacham   Surety: Wilson Walker

EZELL, Baalam   Elizabeth Mayes
    M.B. December 27, 1803   M. December 28, 1803
    Minister: William Richards   Surety: Thomas Owen

EZELL, Baalam, Jr.   Sally Childers
    M.B. November 14, 1808   Surety: Baalam Ezell, Sr.
    Consent: Thomas Hamblin, guardian, who stated that
             Sally is under age

EZELL, Berryman   Phebe Hamblin
    M.B. August 8, 1803   Surety: Peter Hamblin
    Consent: Thomas Hamblin, father of Phebe

FARLEY, James   Martha Evans
    M.B. July 26, 1786   M. July 27, 1786
    Minister: John Williams   Surety: Henry Farley
    Consent: James Farley, Sr., father of James
    Consent: Stephen Evans, father of Martha
    Note: James Farley of Amelia County

FARMER, Thomas   Susanna Stone
    M.B. December 9, 1804   Surety: Jordan Stone

FARRAR, Abel   Sarah Clark
    M.B. August 11, 1788   M. August 20, 1788
                        Surety: Matthew Lancaster Easter
    Minister: Edward Almand

FARRAR, George   Elizabeth Boyd
    M.B. August 22, 1783   Surety: Richard Swepson, Jr.

FARRAR, John   Ann Baskervill
    M.B. December 24, 1794   Surety: Robert Baskervill

FARRAR, John   Nancy Hunt
    M.B. June 13, 1808   M. John P. Finch

FARRAR, Richardson   Susanna Baskervill
    M.B. June 12, 1810   Surety: Newman Dortch

FARRAR, Samuel   Elizabeth Phillips
    M.B. November 10, 1786   Surety: Hardy Jones

FARRAR, Thomas   Sarah Farrar
    M.B. December 13, 1790   Surety: James Faucet

FARRAR, William   Lucy Medley
    M.B. July 24, 1780   Surety: John Farrar

FAULKNER, Johnson   Mary Griffin
    M.B. April 8, 1799   Surety: Stephen P'Pool
    Consent: William Griffin, father of Mary

FEAGINS, John   Patty Lanier
    M.B. January 5, 1786   M. January 7, 1786
    Minister: John King   Surety: John Saunders

FEAGINS, Richardson   Martha Apperson
    M.B. February 3, 1779   Surety: Thomas Pinson
    Consent: David Apperson, father of Martha

FEILD, Edmund   Mary Tanner
    M.B. September 14, 1807   M. September 19, 1807
    Minister: James Meacham   Surety: G. H. Baskervill

FEILD, James   Henryetta Maria Anderson
    M.B. February 17, 1789   Surety: Thomas Anderson, Jr.
    Note: Henrietta, daughter of Thomas Anderson, Sr.

FEILD, John Shaw   Jane Walker
    M.B. June 9, 1788   Surety: Henry Walker
    Minister: Thomas Scott
    Note: Jane, daughter of Henry Walker

FEILD, Thomas   Mary White
    M.B. January 11, 1782   Surety: James Anderson

FARGESON, Joseph *   Elizabeth Holloway
    M.B. February 6, 1789   Surety: Benjamin Ferrell

FARGESON, Peter T. *   Elizabeth Jackson
    M.B. July 5, 1809   Cavil Jackson
    * Name now spelled Ferguson

FERRELL, Benjamin   Mary Burton
    M.B. March 12, 1770   Surety: James Ferrell

FERRELL, Benjamin   Sarah Collier
    M.B. December 13, 1773   Surety: Howell Collier

FERRELL, Benjamin   Ann Dortch
    M.B. February 11, 1784   Surety: William Baskervill

FERRELL, William   Dolly Bailey
    M.B. April 9, 1795   Surety: James Ferrell
    Minister: William Creath
    Note: William Ferrell of Halifax County

FINCH, Edward   Jane Puryear
    M.B. March 13, 1775   Surety: John Puryear

FINCH, George   Janey Short
    M.B. December 7, 1796   M. December 21, 1796
    Minister: John Loyd   Surety: Freeman Short

FINCH, George   Amy Arnold
    M.B. September 22, 1803   Surety: Jeremiah Arnold

FINCH, Henry   Martha Steagall
    M.B. June 2, 1794   Surety: Robert Pennington

FINCH, John   Elizabeth Farrar
    M.B. April 18, 1787   Surety: Peter Farrar
    Consent: John Farrar, father of Elizabeth

FINCH, John P.   Nancy Graves
    M.B. September 14, 1795   Elijah Graves
    Minister: William Creath

FINCH, William   Rebecca Clay
    M.B. August 14, 1775   Surety: Edward Finch
    Consent: Henry Clay, relation not stated

FINCH, William   Elizabeth Christopher
    M.B. January 31, 1780   Surety: William Christopher
    Note: Elizabeth, daughter of David Christopher

FISHER, Jonathon   Susannah Booth
    M.B. May 5, 1801   Surety: Reuben Booth
    Minister: James Meacham

FLOOD, William   Molly Harris Brogdon
  M.B. November 12, 1785   Surety: Thomas Macklin
  Consent: William Brogdon (relation not stated) who
     says Molly Brogdon is 21 years old

FLOYD, Drury   Betsy Lanier
  M.B. October 25, 1791   M. October 27, 1791
  Minister: John Loyd   Surety: Josiah Floyd
  Consent: Lemuel Lanier, father of Betsy

FLOYD, Josiah   Rebecca Bugg
  M.B. March 28, 1810   Surety: Jesse Bugg

FLYNNE, John   Sarah Green
  M.B. April 11, 1791   Surety: David Green
  Minister: Henry Ogburn

FONTAINE, Joseph   Mary Goode
  M.B. February 8, 1773   Edward Goode

FOWLER, Starling   Sarah Ellis
  M.B. December 4, 1802   M. December 8, 1802
  Minister: James Meacham Surety: Jesse Perkinson

FOX, Benjamin   Martha Nowell
  M.B. May 29, 1792   M. June 9, 1792
  Minister: William Creath Surety: Young Nowell

FOX, Richard   Mary Rainey
  M.B. March 22, 1775   Surety: William Davis

FOX, Richard   Nancy Wright
  M.B. October 4, 1792   Surety: Solomon Patillo

FOX, Robert   Polly Warren
  M.B. November 26, 1801   Surety: John Warren

FRANCIS, John   Elizabeth Epperson
  M.B. September 8, 1794   M. November 1, 1794
  Minister: William Richards Surety: Joseph Townes

FRASAR, John   Lucy Adams
  M.B. January 4, 1780 Surety: William Crutchfield
  Note: John Frasar of Prince Edward County
  Note: Lucy, daughter of Thomas and Lucy Adams

FRASER, Daniel   * Martha Fargeson
  M.B. February 14, 1805   Surety: John Fraser
  * Martha Ferguson

FRAZER, James   * Happy Brame
    M.B. June 3, 1778   Surety: John Brame
    * Kerrenhappuck Brame
    Note: James Frazer of Orange County, N. C.
    Note: Kerrenhappuck, daughter of Richins Brame

FREEMAN, Benjamin   Mary Roberts
    M.B. May 26, 1803   Surety: Stephen Roberts
    Minister: William Creath

FREEMAN, Gideon   Mary Elam
    M.B. January 10, 1803   M. January 19, 1803
    Minister: William Richards   Surety: Philemon Hurt

FREEMAN, John   Polly Allen
    M.B. December 13, 1796   M. December 22, 1796
    Minister: William Richards   Surety: Thomas Allen

FREEMAN, John   Lucy Hudson
    M.B. October 9, 1798   M. October 11, 1798
    Minister: William Richards   Surety: Stephen Hudson
    Consent: George Freeman, father of John

FREEMAN, John   * Agga Walker
    M.B. July 22, 1806   Surety: John Johnson
    * Agatha Walker

GABARD, John   Betsey Curtis
    M.B. February 25, 1792   M. February 28, 1792
    Minister: John Loyd   Surety: Ely Curtis

GARLAND, Capt. Thomas   Polly Lowry
    M.B. July 8, 1783   Surety: John Speed
    Consent: John Ragsdale, guardian of Polly Lowry
    Note: Captain Thomas Garland of Lunenburg County

GARNER, James   Lucy Eddins
    M.B. January 11, 1790   Surety: Thomas Dance
    Minister: Edward Almand

GARNER, James   Mary Smith
    M.B. November 10, 1806   M. November 20, 1806
    Minister: William Richards   Surety: Hume R. Feild

GARNER, Vinson   Nancy Jeffries
    M.B. November 9, 1807   M. November 12, 1807
    Minister: William Richards   Surety: Richard Jeffries

GARRETT, Jacob   Hannah Pettyford
     M.B. November 4, 1802   M. November 6, 1802
     Minister: William Richards   Surety: Drury Pettyford

GARROTT, William   Mary Roberts
     M.B. November 9, 1795   Surety: Thomas Massey
     Minister: William Creath

GAYLE, John   Nancy Whitehead
     M.B. March 23, 1793   M. March 26, 1793
     Minister: William Creath   Surety: William Whitehead
     Note: John Gayle of Halifax County

GEE, James   Lucy Bugg
     M.B. February 6, 1797   M. February 16, 1797
     Minister: John Loyd   Surety: John Bugg
     Consent: Nevil Gee, father of James
     Note: James Gee of Lunenburg County

GEE, James Street   Nancy Gee
     M.B. November 10, 1798   M. November 14, 1798
     Minister: William Creath   Surety: Jones Gee

GEE, Jeremiah   Betsey Andrews
     M.B. November 19, 1804   Surety: Varney Andrews
     Note: Elizabeth Andrews, called Betsey, daughter of
         Varney Andrews, Sr.

GEE, Nevil   Elizabeth Andrews
     M.B. July 19, 1797   M. July 20, 1797
     Minister: Charles Ogburn   Surety: Varney Andrews
     Consent: Nevil Gee, Sr., father of Nevil
     Consent: George Andrews, father of Elizabeth
     Note: Elizabeth (Andrews) Gee married (2) Peter
         Burton

GEE, Peter R.   Elizabeth H. Daly
     M.B. January 18, 1808   Surety: Tignal Abernathy

GEE, William   Caty Jones
     M.B. December 12, 1787   Surety: Varney Andrews
     Note: William Gee of Lunenburg County

GEORGE, Jeremiah   Mary Lambert
     M.B. June 6, 1797   Surety: Thomas Lambert

GILES, Edward   Martha Ezell
     M.B. January 31, 1801   Surety: Thomas Nance

GILES, Edward   Angelica Mabry
     M.B. January 3, 1810   Surety: Walter Pennington
     Consent: Stephen Mabry, father of Angelica

GILES, William   Lucy Standley
    M.B. December 17, 1804   Surety: James Standley

GILL, Metcalf   Sukey Cole
    M.B. June 4, 1799   Surety: John Allgood

GILL, William   Judith Maynard
    M.B. December 8, 1783   Surety: Nicholas Maynard

GILLESPIE, Martin   Elizabeth Elam
    M.B. February 10, 1806   M. February 20, 1806
    Minister: William Richards   Surety: Henry H. Dedman

GLASGOW, Richard   Amey Chappell
    M.B. December 28, 1785   Surety: Philip Reekes

GLASGOW, William   Lockey Avery
    M.B. February 1, 1800   Surety: Richard Glasgow

GLIDEWELL, John   Anne Whitlow
    M.B. August 20, 1785   M. September 30, 1785
    Minister: John Williams   Surety: Thomas Whitlow

GLOVER, Daniel   Mary Westmoreland
    M.B. November 8, 1806   Surety: Robert Westmoreland

GOEN, Frederick *   Susey Chavous
    M.B. March 9, 1789   Surety: Frederick Ivey
    Consent: Henry Chavous, Sr., father of Susey
    Minister: Phillip Cox

GOEN, Frederick *   Mary Brandon
    M.B. December 29, 1800   M. January 1, 1801
    Minister: William Richards   Surety: Ephraim Drew
    * Return of minister says Gowen

GOLD, Ephraim   Jane Hailey
    M.B. July 8, 1799   Surety: Elijah Griffin
    Consent: Thomas Hailey, father of Jane
    Minister: William Creath

GOOCH, Joseph   Anne Lockett
    M.B. June 27, 1794   Surety: William Marshall
    Note: nee Anne Marshall, widow of Abner Lockett
    Note: Joseph Gooch of Granville County, N. C.

GOODE, Edward   Joice Holmes
    M.B. December 13, 1798   M. December 18, 1798
    Minister: Charles Ogburn   Surety: Richard Cox
    Note: Joice, daughter of Samuel Holmes

GOODE, John   Martha Moore
    M.B. April 19, 1790   Surety: John Wilson, Jr.

GOODE, John   Rebecca J. Pully
    M.B. July 18, 1796   Surety: John Dortch

GOODE, John   Mary Jones
    M.B. May 8, 1809   M. May 11, 1809
    Minister: William Richards   Surety: William G. Goode

GOODE, John B.   Permelia B. Hendrick
    M.B. July 2, 1804   M. July 4, 1804
    Minister: James Meacham   Surety: Amasa Palmer

GOODE, Joseph   Martha Birtchett
    M.B. August 31, 1790   Surety: Philip Morgan

GOODE, Richard   Nancy Charlotte Poindexter
    M.B. October 8, 1781   Surety: Phil Poindexter, Jr.
    Consent: Philip Poindexter, Sr., father of Nancy

GOODE, Samuel   Mary Armistead Burwell
    M.B. September 28, 1786   Surety: Nicholas Bilbo
    Consent: Lewis Burwell, father of Mary

GOODE, William G.   Mary Tabb
    M.B. September 2, 1798   M. September 4, 1798
    Minister: Alexander Hay   Surety: G. H. Baskervill

GOODWIN, Beal   Elizabeth Frazer
    M.B. December 10, 1798   M. January 29, 1799
    Minister: William Richards   Surety: James Brame
    Consent: Henry Frazer, father of Elizabeth

GOODWIN, Samuel   Lucy Smith
    M.B. March 22, 1793   Surety: Thomas Hord
    Consent: Mary Hord, mother of Lucy Smith *
    Note: Lucy, daughter of Drury Smith, deceased
    Note: Samuel Goodwin of Bottetourt County
    * Mary Smith, widow of Drury Smith, married (2) John
      Camp and (3) Thomas Hord

GRAVES, Frederick   Nancy Brandon
    M.B. December 29, 1800   Surety: Ephraim Drew

GRAVES, Howell   Elizabeth Hunt
    M.B. April 13, 1801   Surety: James Hunt

GRAVES, Ralph   Elizabeth Graves
    M.B. February 9, 1789   Surety: Henry Walker

GRAVES, Thomas   Mary Harris
    M.B. December 26, 1808   M. December 27, 1808
    Minister: William Richards   Surety: John Stembridge

GRAVES, William   Anne Neal
    M.B. _____   *
    Minister: James Read
    * Marriage Bond does not give name of surety or date

GRAVES, William   Frances Elam
    M.B. October 14, 1795   M. October 20, 1795
    Minister: William Richards   Surety: Thomas Graves

GREEN, Abraham   Ann Coleman
    M.B. March 2, 1799   M. March 14, 1799
    Minister: William Creath   Surety: James W. Oliver

GREEN, Archibald   Judith Taylor
    M.B. October 11, 1802   M. November 9, 1802
    Minister: F. S. Stewart   Surety: Thomas Rowlett

GREEN, Henry   Molly Vaughan
    M.B. August 2, 1799   Surety: Stephen P'Pool

GREEN, James   Nancy Yancey
    M.B. January 9, 1792   M. January 11, 1792
    Minister: James Read   Surety: William Hendrick

GREEN, Lewis   Elizabeth Crawley
    M.B. September 8, 1788   Surety: John Baskervill
    Minister: Thomas Scott

GREEN, Thomas   Francinia Cox
    M.B. March 22, 1792   M. April 5, 1792
    Minister: John Williams   Surety: John Cox, Jr.
    Note: Thomas Green of Lunenburg County

GREEN, William W.   Mary Poindexter
    M.B. January 3, 1803   M. January 11, 1803
    Minister: Mattew Dance   Surety: G. H. Baskervill
    Note: Mary Poindexter, nee Mary Hinton, widow of
          Phillip Poindexter, Jr.

GREENWOOD, James   Jane Saunders
    M.B. May 10, 1779   Surety: James Hall

GREENWOOD, James   Henrietta Hester
    M.B. June 9, 1794   M. June 11, 1794
    Minister: William Richards   Surety: Henry H. Dedman
    Consent: James Hester, uncle of Henrietta Hester
    Note: Henrietta, daughter of Abraham Hester, deceased

GREENWOOD, Thomas, Jr.   Martha Williams
    M.B. October 8, 1792   M. October 25, 1792
    Minister: William Creath   Surety: James T. Hayes

GREGORY, Banister   Susanna Griffin
    M.B. August 29, 1808   Surety: Elijah Griffin
    Consent: John Gregory, relation not stated

GREGORY, Elijah   Nancy Moody
    M.B. June 8, 1801   M. June 10, 1801
    Minister: William Richards   Surety: Robert Smith

GREGORY, James   Sarah Doggett
    M.B. September 14, 1801   M. October 1, 1801
    Minister: William Richards   Surety: John Swansbow

GREGORY, John   Polly Apperson
    M.B. December 19, 1786   M. December 23, 1786
    Minister: Henry Lester   Surety: John Apperson
    Consent: David Apperson, father of Polly

GREGORY, Nathaniel   Mary Ann Beckley
    M.B. January ___, 1787 *   Surety: Edward L. Tabb
    * Day of month not given on bond

GREGORY, Robert S.   Letty Couch
    M.B. August 14, 1809   M. August 26, 1809
    Minister: William Richards   Surety: John Couch

GREGORY, Roger, Jr.   Elizabeth Speed
    M.B. October 21, 1791   Surety: Sherwood Bugg

GRESHAM, Gregory   Susannah Smith
    M.B. July 23, 1806   Surety: Thomas Smith
    Consent: William Smith, father of Susannah
    Consent: Asa Gresham, Sr., father of Gregory

GRIFFIN, James   Polly Tindal
    M.B. December 14, 1807   Surety: Overton Wiles

GRIFFIN, John   Elizabeth Yancey
    M.B. August 11, 1794   Surety: Robert Williamson

GRIFFIN, William   Edna Blanks
    M.B. September 26, 1803   Surety: Joseph Blanks

GRIFFITH, John   Rainey Rottenbury
    M.B. December 14, 1790   M. December 16, 1790
    Minister: John King   Surety: John Lambert
    Consent: John Griffith, Sr., father of John

GRIGG, Burwell   Labia Elam
    M.B. October 8, 1787   Surety: Alexander Elam
    Minister: John Williams

GRIGG, Drury   Anna Chavous
    M.B. April 13, 1807   Surety: Saunders Harris

GRIGG, Jesse   Martha Elam
    M.B. December 11, 1786   Surety: James Elam

GRIGG, Lewis   Patsy Malone
    M.B. March 30, 1808   Surety: Thomas Cleaton

GRIGG, Randolph   Elizabeth Jordan
    M.B. December 13, 1805   Surety: Samuel Jordan
    Consent: Mary Jordan, mother of Elizabeth

GRIGG, William   Mary M. Jordan
    M.B. December 8, 1800   M. December 11, 1800
    Minister: James Meacham   Surety: John Matthews

GRYMES, Benjamin   Ann Nicholas, Spinster
    M.B. December 22, 1778   Surety: John Nicholas

GWALTNEY, John   Lucy Bowen
    M.B. February 12, 1798   Surety: Micajah Gwaltney
    Minister: Charles Ogburn

GWALTNEY, John   * Willie Underwood
    M.B. December 4, 1806   M. December 5, 1806
    Minister: Matthew Dance   Surety: William Gwaltney
    * Wilhelmina Underwood

GWALTNEY, William   Agness Colley
    M.B. May 23, 1801   Surety: James Brown

GUY, Daniel   Nancy Erby
    M.B. February 26, 1806   Surety: William Chandler

GUY, George   Nancy Drew
    M.B. December 11, 1799   M. December 12, 1799
    Minister: Ebenezer Macgowan   Surety: William Chandler

HAILE, Dudley   Mary Willis
    M.B. December 1781   Surety: Thomas Haile

HAILE, Dudley   Susanna Smith
    M.B. February 10, 1794   Surety: Harrison Winn

HAILE, Dudley   Patsy Carter
    M.B. January 12, 1795   Surety: William Willis

HAILE, Leman   Elizabeth Avory
    M.B. June 19, 1802   Surety: Elijah Avory
    Minister: William Creath

HAILE, Thomas   Sally Rudd
   M.B. December 17, 1804   M. December 19, 1804
   Minister: William Richards   Surety: Harwood Rudd

HAILE, Thomas   Nancy Blacketter
   M.B. September 25, 1805   Surety: Harwood Rudd

HAILEY, David   Lucy Crow
   M.B. December 3, 1804   Surety: Jachonias Towler

HALEY, David   Elizabeth Brooks
   M.B. December 8, 1783   Surety: Elijah Graves

HALEY, John   Dycy Blanks
   M.B. July 8, 1799   Surety: Elijah Griffin
   Consent: Joseph Blanks, father of Dicey

HALEY, Richard   Nancy Wilson
   M.B. January 26, 1805   Surety: John E. Harris
   Minister: William Creath

HALEY, Thomas *   Elizabeth Gold
   M.B. June 9, 1794   M. June 12, 1794
   Minister: James Read   Surety: Daniel Gold, Jr.
   Note: Elizabeth, widow of Daniel Gold, Sr.
   * Name spelled Hailey in later records

HALL, Miles   Susanna Marshall
   M.B. May 4, 1781   Surety: Richard Winn
   Consent: James Hall, father of Miles
   Consent: Dancy McCraw, guardian of Susanna

HALL, Miles   Nancy Cox
   M.B. September 8, 1806   M. September 18, 1806
   Minister: William Richards   Surety: John Cox

HALL, Richard Carter   Elizabeth Mayes
   M.B. August 11, 1794   Surety: John Hall
   Consent: John Mayes, father of Elizabeth

HALL, William   Elizabeth Bradley
   M.B. December 6, 1802   Surety: John Bradley

HALL, Zachariah   Sophia Malone
   M.B. December 4, 1792   M. December 5, 1792
   Minister: John Loyd   Surety: Thomas Roberts

HAMBLIN, John   Milly Daniel
   M.B. July 13, 1807   Surety: Stephen Stone
   Consent: Martin Daniel, father of Milly

HAMBLIN, Thomas   Jean Childress
    M.B. November 10, 1806   Surety: Baalam Ezell

HAMILTON, Andrew   Elizabeth Skinner
    M.B. February 14, 1782   Surety: Josiah Daly
    Note: Andrew Hamilton of Prince George County

HAMILTON, Baxter   Prissey Bailey
    M.B. January 10, 1798   Surety: Robert Roberts
    Minister: William Creath

HAMILTON, John   Polly Hatsell
    M.B. January 12, 1795   Surety: Stephen Hatsell

HAMILTON, Joseph   Sarah Cox
    M.B. May 16, 1791   Surety: Edward Hatsell

HAMILTON, Walter   Elizabeth Hatsell
    M.B. August 24, 1785   Surety: Mary Hatsell

HAMILTON, William   Nancy Christopher
    M.B. January 14, 1799   Surety: William Christopher

HAMLETT, William   Mary Brooke
    M.B. October 27, 1789   Surety: Gabriel Carleton
    Note: William Hamlett of Halifax County

HAMLIN, Charles   Susanna Owen
    Minister: Henry Lester   M. April 24, 1785

HAMLIN, William B.   Christian Burwell
    M.B. December 18, 1794   Surety: Daniel Mayes
    Consent: Mary Hamlin, mother of William
    Consent: Lewis Burwell, father of Christian
    Note: Daniel Mayes of Dinwiddie County

HAMME, Frederick   Elizabeth D. Butler
    M.B. March 12, 1804   Surety: John White
    Minister: Matthew Dance   M. March 22, 1804

HAMMOND, Frederick   Polly Stewart
    M.B. August 14, 1807   M. September 4, 1807
    Minister: William Richards   Surety: Frederick Dyson

HAMNER, George B.   Anne Edmundson
    M.B. December 16, 1793   M. December 19, 1793
    Minister: William Creath   Surety: Banister Edmundson
    Consent: Samuel Edmundson, father of Anne

HAMNER, John   Molly Whobery
    M.B. December 22, 1790   Surety: John Whobery

57

HANSERD, Richard   Sarah Speed
    M.B. December 12, 1774   Surety: Robert Ballard

HANSERD, Richard   Sarah Ferguson
    M.B. June 18, 1801   Surety: John Dortch
    Minister: James Meacham

HARDY, James   Mary Wilson
    M.B. January 12, 1801   Surety: John Boswell

HARGROVE, Burnett   Biddy Lambert
    M.B. January 23, 1788   Surety: Matthew Smith

HARGROVE, James   Nancy Thomas
    M.B. December 14, 1797   Surety: John Thomas

HARPER, John   Martha Pennington
    M.B. December 7, 1785 Surety: John George Pennington
    Consent: John Harper, Sr., father of John

HARPER, Thomas   Lucy Gillam Booth
    M.B. January 22, 1791   M. February 10, 1791
    Minister: Henry Ogburn   Surety: Thomas Booth
    Note: Thomas Harper of Dinwiddie County

HARPER, Wyatt   Mary M, Pennington
    M.B. July 29, 1799   M. July 30, 1799
    Minister: John Neblett   Surety: William Pennington

HARRIS, Allen   Susanna Harris
    M.B. March 1, 1800   Surety: James Reamy
    Minister: William Richards   M. March 4, 1800
    Consent: Reuben Harris, father of Susanna

HARRIS, Drury   Patsy Butler
    M.B. October 10, 1803   Surety: Charles Carter
    Consent: John Butler, Sr., father of Patsy

HARRIS, Henry   Polly Roper
    M.B. October 20, 1809   Surety: Willson Harris

HARRIS, Ivey   Judith Allgood
    M.B. December __, 1809 *   Surety: John Allgood
    * Day of month not given on bond

HARRIS, James   Rebecca Nolley
    M.B. December 20, 1806   Surety: Nevison Nolley

HARRIS, Jeremiah   Lydia Chavous
    M.B. November 13, 1797   M. November 27, 1797
    Minister: Matthew L. Easter   Surety: James Chavous

HARRIS, John   Sarah Berry
    M.B. December 25, 1786   Surety: George Hudson

HARRIS, John   Rittah Stewart
    M.B. December 27, 1802   Surety: Jeremiah Harris

HARRIS, John   Martha Crutchfield
    M.B. December 19, 1803   Surety: William Crutchfield

HARRIS, Mastin   Patsy Reamey
    M.B. December 14, 1807   Surety: William Harris
    Minister: William Richards   M. December 18, 1807
    Note: Mastin, Son of James and Martha Harris, and
           grandson of William and Judith Harris

HARRIS, Reuben   Sarah Matthews
    M.B. December 20, 1808   Surety: John Cook

HARRIS, Robert   Mary White
    M.B. January 10, 1791   William White
    Minister: James Read

HARRIS, Sherwood   Joannah Ragsdale
    M.B. October 25, 1800   Surety: Robert Ragsdale
    Minister: William Richards   M. November 1, 1800
    Note: Sherwood, son of William Harris, Junr.

HARRIS, Thomas   Elizabeth Graves
    M.B. December 28, 1795   M. January 3, 1796
    Minister: Edward Almand   Surety: Peter Elam

HARRIS, William   Mary I. Elam
    M.B. September 27, 1799   Surety: Daniel Wilson
    Consent: Barkley Elam, father of Mary

HARRIS, William W.   Clary Hudson
    M.B. June 14, 1802   Surety: William Hudson
    Minister: William Richards

HARRIS, William   Anna Reamy
    M.B. November 12, 1804   M. December 20, 1804
    Minister: Edward Almand   Surety: Abraham Reamy
    Consent: James Reamy, father of Anna

HARRISON, Greenwood   Susannah Mullins
    M.B. February 11, 1799   M. March 14, 1799
    Minister: William Richards   Surety: Edward Holloway

HARRISON, James   Tabitha Webb
    M.B. December 5, 1801   M. December 8, 1801
    Minister: James Meacham   Surety: Abdias P. Webb
    Consent: E. Webb, father of Tabitha

HARRISON, John   Betsy Lelilah Parham
    M.B. March 22, 1792   M. March 27, 1792
    Minister: Edward Dromgoole   Surety: William Kirks
    Note: John Harrison of Northampton County, N. C.
    Note: William Kirks of Orange County, N. C.

HARRISON, Robert   Martha Baugh
    M.B. January 19, 1787   Surety: William Baugh
    Note: Martha, daughter of James and Agnes Baugh

HARRISON, William   Margaret Wade
    M.B. November 16, 1790   Surety: Absolóm Hasting

HARWELL, Samuel   Martha Harwell
    M.B. December 18, 1804   Surety: William Harwell
    Consent: James Harwell, relation not stated

HASTIN, Absolom   Patsy Wade
    M.B. January 12, 1789   M. January 22, 1789
    Minister: Edward Almand   Surety: John Wagstaff

HASTIN, Henry   Fanny W. Graves
    M.B. June 19, 1799   M. June 20, 1799
    Minister: William Richards   Surety: Thomas Graves

HASTIN, John   Nancy Elam
    M.B. October 8, 1787   Surety: Absolom Hastin

HATCHELL, Stephen   Nancy Roberts
    M.B. November 12, 1792   M. November 15, 1792
    Minister: John Loyd   Surety: William Nanney

HATSELL, Edward   Sarah Cox
    M.B. March 16, 1804   Surety: Stephen Hatsell

HATSELL, John   Prudence Halton
    M.B. February 17, 1786   Surety: William Baskervill

HATSELL, John   Aggy Smith
    M.B. April 5, 1786   * Surety: John Lollis
    * John Lawless ?

HAWKINS, Claiborne   Margaret Barry
    M.B. May 2, 1789   Surety: Frederick Andrews
    Minister: Thomas Scott

HAWKINS, Green   Mourning Carroll
    M.B. December 27, 1802   Surety: Mark L. Jackson

HAWKINS, John   Elizabeth Goode
    M.B. December 19, 1785   Surety: Robert Goode
    Consent: Edward Goode, father of Elizabeth

HAWKINS, John D.   Jane A. Boyd
    M.B. April 11, 1803   Surety : Richard Boyd
    Minister: John Cameron

HAWKINS, Phil   Lucy Davis
    M.B. August 22, 1775   Surety: William Davis
    Note: Lucy, daughter of William Davis
    Note: Phil Hawkins of Bute County, N. C.

HAWKINS, Uriah   Lucy Green Jones
    M.B. March 7, 1798   Surety: William Jones
    Minister: Ebenezer Macgowan

HAWKINS, William   Nancy Boyd
    M.B. December 12, 1803   Surety: Richard Boyd
    Minister: John Cameron

HAWKS, Joseph   Phoebe Westbrook
    M.B. May 13, 1799   Surety: Thomas Westbrook
    Minister: Charles Ogburn

HAYES, Hyram   Phebe Hill
    M.B. August 8, 1791   M. August 10, 1791
    Minister: John Williams   Surety: Nicholas Jeter

HAYES, James   Patsy Green
    M.B. March 22, 1806   M. March 25, 1806
    Minister: James Meacham   M. James T. Hayes
    Consent: William Wills Green, father of Patsy

HAYES, James Toy   Mary Puryear
    M.B. December 23, 1791   M. December 29, 1791
    Minister: William Creath   Surety: Reuben Puryear

HAYES, John Jr.   Catey Decker
    M.B. August 19, 1794   Surety: William Decker

HAYLES, John   Mary Sullivant
    M.B. May 26, 1783   Surety: William Baskervill

HAYNES, George   Sarah Gregory
    M.B. February 9, 1795   Surety: Joseph Gregory
    Note: George Haynes of Charlotte County

HAZLEWOOD, Daniel   Lucy Waller
    M.B. August 2, 1803   Surety: John Waller
    Minister: William Creath

HEARN, John   Elizabeth Hill Whitby
    M.B. December 18, 1793   M. December 19, 1793
    Minister: John Loyd   Surety: Nathaniel Chambers
    Consent: Mary Crowder, mother of Elizabeth Whitby

HEGGIE, John   Mary Ann Hunt
    M.B. August 29, 1807   Surety: Absolom Hunt
    Consent: James Hunt, father of Mary Ann

HENDRICK, John   Edith King
    M.B. October 25, 1800   Surety: Henry King

HENDRICK, Thomas   Sally Wall
    M.B. December 12, 1803   Surety: Charles Hamblin

HENDRICK, William   Susannah Crews
    M.B. March 8, 1772   Surety: John Atkinson

HENDRICK, William   Rebecca Wall
    M.B. February 11, 1805   Surety: Howell Graves

HEPBURN, William   Mary Watts McHarg
    M.B. September 12, 1785   Surety: George Tarry

HESTER, Francis   Ann Greenwood
    M.B. December 13, 1779   Surety: James Hester
    Consent: Thomas Greenwood, father of Ann
    Note: James Hester, brother of Francis
    Note: Francis, son of Robert and Barbara Hester of
          Louisa County

HESTER, James   Elizabeth Hix
    M.B. September 4, 1767   Surety: Amos Hix
    Note: James, son of Robert and Barbara Hester of
          Louisa County

HESTER, Robert   Nancy Lockett
    M.B. February 13, 1792   M. February 28, 1792
    Minister: James Read   Surety: John Wilson

HESTER, Robert   Mary Crowder
    M.B. July 29, 1795   M. August 1, 1795
    Minister: William Richards Surety: Robert Hester,Sr.

HESTER, Robert   Susannah Garner
    M.B. January 11, 1802   Surety: Richard Swepson

HESTER, Robert   Lucy Culbreath
    M.B. January 12, 1807   Surety: John Farrar

HESTER, Samuel   Elizabeth Greenwood
    M.B. November 8, 1784   Surety: Caleb Johnston
    Consent: Thomas Greenwood, father of Elizabeth
    Note: Samuel, son of Robert and Barbara Hester of
          Louisa County

HETHCOCK, Whittemore   Henrietta Ladd
    M.B. November 26, 1808   Surety: James Drumwright

HICKS, Benjamin   Lucy Brooking
    M.B. June 15, 1786   Surety: William Lucas
    Note: Benjamin Hicks of Chesterfield County, S.C.

HICKS, Daniel   Frances Delony
    M.B. September 18, 1788   Surety: William Delony
    Note: Frances, daughter of Henry Delony

HICKS, David   Nancy Thompson
    M.B. January 23, 1795   M. January 31, 1795
    Minister: John Loyd   Surety: George Thompson

HICKS, Isaac   Frances Lucas
    M.B. March 10, 1807   Surety: John R. Lucas

HICKS, Jacob   Jincy Gordon
    M.B. October 31, 1794   M. November 6, 1794
    Minister: John Loyd   Surety: Arthur F. Winfield

HICKS, John   Gracey Coleman
    M.B. June 22, 1789   Surety: Pettus Phillips
    Minister: Thomas Scott
    Note: Grace, daughter of Cluverius Coleman

HIGHTOWER, Devereaux   Susanna Hutcheson
    M.B. August 18, 1800   Surety: Joseph Hutcheson
    Consent: Charles Hutcheson, father of Susanna
    Minister: William Creath

HIGHTOWER, Stephen   Tabitha Baugh
    M.B. July 16, 1808   Surety: Richard Baugh
    Note: Tabitha, daughter of James and Agnes Baugh

HILL, Edward   Jemima Blankenship
    M.B. July 28, 1802   Surety: John Webb

HILL, John   Elizabeth Marshall
    M.B. February 20, 1799   M. February 27, 1799
    Minister: William Richards   Surety: John Dortch
    Consent: Robert Marshall, father of Elizabeth

HILL, Richard   Nancy Phillips
    M.B. January 29, 1800   Surety: William Brown
    Consent: Dabney Phillips, Sr., father of Nancy

HILL, Richard   Sally Burnett
    M.B. July 17, 1806   M. August 11, 1806
    Minister: Thomas Hardie   Surety: Jesse Burnett

HILL, William   Ann Freeman Wagstaff
     M.B. June 8, 1789   M. June 17, 1789
     Minister: John Williams   Surety: Britain Wagstaff

HILTON, William   Jincy Hutt
     M.B. February 10, 1800   Surety: Thomas Hutt
     Minister: William Creath

HINTON, Presley   Elizabeth Worsham
     M.B. January 10, 1801   M. January 14, 1801
     Minister: James Meacham   Surety: William Blanton

HITE, Vincent   Nancy Wilborn
     M.B. December 14, 1807   Surety: Thomas Wilborn
     Consent: John Wilborn, father of Nancy

HIX, Daniel   Susannah Jeffries
     M.B. April 12, 1784   Surety: John Jeffries

HIX, Jesse   Sarah Bugg
     M.B. November 26, 1774   Surety: Samuel Bugg
     Note: Sarah, daughter of Samuel (Sr.) and Martha Bugg

HIX, Nathaniel   Frances Burton
     M.B. October 9, 1783   Surety: Sherwood Bugg
     Note: Nathaniel Hix of Georgia
     Note: Sherwood Bugg, son of Samuel (Sr.) and Martha
          Bugg

HIX, Sherwood   Ann Gordon
     M.B. January 18, 1782   Surety: Walter Leigh

HIX, Thomas   Elizabeth Bevill
     M.B. December 13, 1796   Surety: Francis Neal
     Minister: William Creath

HODGE, John   Jane Thornton
     M.B. October 24, 1787   Surety: Hugh B. Nanney

HOLCOMB, Philemon   Lucy Anderson
     M.B. December 13, 1784   Surety: Charles Lewis
     Note: Philemon Holcomb of Prince Edward County
     Note: Lucy, daughter of Thomas and Sarah Anderson

HOLLOWAY, Anderson   Susanna Gillespie
     M.B. July 1, 1799   M. July 2, 1799
     Minister: William Richards   Surety: John Dortch

HOLLOWAY, David   Mary Wright
     M.B. December 21, 1799   M. December 24, 1799
     Minister: Ebenezer Macgowan   Surety: John Holmes

HOLLOWAY, Edward   Nancy Farrar
    M.B. November 8, 1806   M. November 11, 1806
    Minister: James Meacham   Surety: Francis Ballard

HOLLOWAY, George   Anne Hall
    M.B. October 24, 1774   Surety: William Holloway
    Consent: James Hall, father of Anne

HOLLOWAY, Gray   Maryanna Baker
    M.B. January 24, 1801   Surety: William Holloway

HOLLOWAY, John   Ann Starling
    M.B. December 17, 1793   Surety: Richard Hanserd
    Consent: William Starling, father of Ann

HOLLOWAY, John   Frances Crowder
    M.B. January 12, 1795   M. January 22, 1795
    Minister: William Richards   Surety: Godfrey Crowder

HOLMES, David   Elizabeth Clark
    M.B. January 15, 1790   Surety: Samuel Holmes, Jr.
    Note: David, son of Isaac and Lucy Holmes

HOLMES, David   Creasy Seward
    M.B. January 1, 1810   Surety: Lemuel Vaughan

HOLMES, Edward   Elizabeth Allen
    M.B. June 17, 1797   M. June 20, 1797
    Minister: Charles Ogburn   Surety: James Jones

HOLMES, John   Mary Taylor
    M.B. December 20, 1779   Surety: Jones Taylor
    Note: John, son of Isaac and Lucy Holmes

HOLMES, John   Milly Turner
    M.B. August 31, 1797   Surety: Matthew Turner, Jr.
    Consent: John Turner, father of Milly

HOLMES, Pennington   Rebecca Daws
    M.B. June 29, 1798   M. July 4, 1798
    Minister: Charles Ogburn   Surety: John Daws

HOLMES, Samuel   Prudence Courtney
    M.B. October 23, 1775   Surety: William Turnbull
    Note: Prudence Courtney, widow of Clack Courtney

HOLMES, Samuel, Jr.   Hannah Fox
    M.B. December 13, 1796   Surety: Edward Holmes
    Consent: William Holmes, Sr., father of Samuel

HOLMES, William   Betsy Crowder
    M.B. February 25, 1783   Surety: Charles Davis

HOLT, Thomas   Lucy Charlotte Blackbourn
     M.B. October 12, 1780   Surety: John Brown
     Note: Thomas Holt of Chesterfield County
     Note: Lucy, daughter of Thomas Blackbourn

HOLT, Thomas B.   Jane Field
     M.B. May 25, 1802   Surety: John Dortch

HOOD, Charles   Sarah Durham
     M.B. June 28, 1786   M. July 15, 1786
     Minister: John Marshall   Surety: James Willis

HOOD, John   Sally Rudd
     M.B. October 8, 1804   M. October 16, 1804
     Minister: James Meacham   Surety: William Birtchett

HOOD, Starling   Martha Vaughan
     M.B. July 11, 1785   Surety: George Barnes
     Consent: Robert Hood, father of Starling

HOOPER, John   Mary Turner
     M.B. July 7, 1806   M. July 10, 1806
     Minister: Charles Ogburn   Surety: Benjamin Reekes

HOPKINS, Edmund   Martha Cary Jones
     M.B. July 25, 1796   M. July 27, 1796
     Minister: William Creath   Surety: John Dortch
     Consent: Tignal Jones, father of Martha

HOPKINS, Samuel (Jr.)   Betty Bugg
     Note: Betty, daughter of Jacob Bugg, Sr.
     M.B. January 18, 1783   Surety: George Nicholas

HORD, James   Martha Puryear
     M.B. November 14, 1803   M. November 24, 1803
     Minister: William Richards   Surety: Thomas Thompson
     Note: James, son of Thomas Hord

HORD, Jesse   Mary C. Erskine
     M.B. February 12, 1798   M. March 15, 1798
     Minister: Edward Almand   Surety: William Christopher
     Note: Jesse, son of Thomas Hord

HORD, Thomas   Mary Camp
     M.B. December 26, 1785   Surety: John Holmes
     Note: Mary, widow of John Camp

HOUSE, John   Sally Evans
     M.B. April 9, 1808   Surety: Labon Short
     Consent: Elizabeth Evans, mother of Sally

HOUSE, Marriott   Polly Short
    M.B. August 23, 1790   Surety: Miles House
    Consent: Jacob Short, father of Polly
    Note: Marriott House of Brunswick County

HOUSE, Miles   Sally Short
    M.B. January 23, 1788   Surety: John Stegall
    Consent: Jacob and Mary Short, parents of Sally
    Note: Miles House of Brunswick County

HUDSON, Benjamin William   Sally Vaughan
    M.B. March 21, 1797   M. March 23, 1797
    Minister: John Loyd Surety: Thos. Chappell Singleton
    Consent: Richard Vaughan, father of Sally

HUDSON, Charles   Nancy Goode
    M.B. December 18, 1790   Surety: Chiles Hutcheson
    Consent: Joseph Goode, father of Nancy

HUDSON, Cuthbert   Lucy Goodwin
    M.B. December 24, 1784   Surety: William Goodwin
    Consent: Peter Goodwin, father of Lucy

HUDSON, David   Sarah Draper
    M.B. December 3, 1789   M. December 5, 1789
    Minister: Edward Almand   Surety: John Hudson

HUDSON, George   Molly Berry
    M.B. December 11, 1786   Surety: William Harris
    Consent: Thomas Berry, father of Molly

HUDSON, Hall   Dicy Allgood
    M.B. November 9, 1801   Surety: John Hudson

HUDSON, Jacob   Sarah Wade
    M.B. September 8, 1788   Surety: William Lancaster
    Minister: John Williams

HUDSON, James   Elizabeth Mullins
    M.B. February 1, 1786   M: February 21, 1786
    Minister: Henry Lester   Surety: Cox Whitlow

HUDSON, John   Rebecca Ezell
    M.B. March 26, 1794   M. March 28, 1794
    Minister: John Loyd   Surety: Thomas Calvery

HUDSON, John   Sally Williams
    M.B. July 14, 1800   Surety: Christopher Robertson
    Minister: William Creath

HUDSON, John   Fanny Bland
    M.B. April 30, 1801   M. May 1, 1801
    Minister: William Creath
                          Surety: Swepson Jeffries, Jr.
    Consent: Samuel Bland, father of Fanny

HUDSON, John   Lucy Tucker
    M.B. December 10, 1804   Surety: Richard Walden

HUDSON, Richard   Patsy Holloway
    M.B. January 14, 1805   M. January 17, 1805
    Minister: William Richards   Surety: Jordan Mason

HUDSON, Richard   Elizabeth Dodson
    M.B. July 30, 1810   M. July 31, 1810
    Minister: James Meacham   Surety: Edward Dodson

HUDSON, Samuel   Nancy White
    M.B. February 8, 1790   M. February 11, 1790
    Minister: Edward Almand   Surety: William White

HUDSON, William   Taffanus Moore
    M.B. March 2, 1787   Surety: John Wagstaff
    Minister: John Williams

HUDSON, William   Jane Puryear
    M.B. November ___, 1803 *   Surety: Peter Puryear
    Minister: William Creath
    * Day of month not given on bond or minister's return

HUDSON, William   Elizabeth Keeton
    M.B. October 8, 1804   Surety: Richard Hudson

HUDSON, Young   Fanny Hutcheson
    M.B. July 9, 1804   M. July 16, 1804
    Minister: James Meacham   Surety: John Pritchett

HUGHES, James   Frances Norment
    M.B. March 13, 1769   Surety: William Norment

HUGHES, Richard   Sally Christopher
    M.B. August 17, 1786   Surety: David Stokes, Jr.
    Note: Sally, daughter of David Christopher, deceased

HUMPHRIES, Benjamin   Mary Keeton
    M.B. November 25, 1788   Surety: Joseph Keeton

HUNDLEY, Cyer   Ann Holmes
    M.B. July 26, 1791   Surety: Isaac Holmes
    Note: Ann, daughter of Samuel Holmes

HUNDLEY, Willis   Joice Lark Taylor
     M.B. September 23, 1809   Surety: Jones Taylor
     Minister: George Micklejohn

HUNT, James   Prudence Loafman
     M.B. September 26, 1801   M. October 20, 1801
     Minister: Edward Almand   Surety: William Graves
     Note: William Graves of Charlotte County

HUNT, Jesse   Polly Wagstaff
     M.B. May 8, 1799   M. May 30, 1799
     Minister: Edward Almand   Surety: William Hunt

HUNT, Samuel Goodwin   Martha Drumwright
     M.B. December 20, 1802   Surety: William Drumwright
     Consent: William Drumwright, father of Martha

HUNT, William, Senr.   Sarah Allgood
     M.B. July 28, 1788   Surety: William Johnson
     Note: Bride signed own consent and stated that she
               was 30 years old

HURT, James   Ermer Vaughan
     M.B. September 11, 1809   Surety: William Burton
     Minister: William Richards

HURT, Moza   Sally Overton
     M.B. November 10, 1808   M. November 27, 1808
     Minister: William Richards   Surety: John Doggett

HURT, William   Betty Hudson
     M.B. July 22, 1790   M. July 27, 1790
     Minister: John Williams   Surety: John Hudson

HUTCHESON, Chiles   Fanny Moss
     M.B. December 23, 1791   M. December 29, 1791
     Minister: William Creath   Surety: William Coleman
     Consent: Ray Moss, father of Fanny

HUTCHESON, John   Sarah Hutcheson
     M.B. November 22, 1786   Surety: Peter Hutcheson
     Consent: Charles Hutcheson, father of Sarah

HUTCHESON, John   Nancy Stone
     M.B. December 9, 1793   M. December 24, 1793
     Minister: William Creath   Surety: William Stone
     Note: Nancy, daughter of William Stone

HUTCHESON, John   Sarah Baugh
     M.B. December 23, 1793   M. January 2, 1794
     Minister: John Loyd   Surety: James Baugh
     Note: Sarah (Sally), daughter of James Baugh

HUTCHESON, John   Molly Suggett
    M.B. August 31, 1801   M. September 1, 1801
    Minister: William Creath   Surety: Samuel Hutcheson

HUTCHESON, Peter   Lilly Wagstaff
    M.B. December 11, 1797   M. December 21, 1797
    Minister: William Richards   Surety: John Wagstaff

HUTCHESON, Richard   Sally Turner
    M.B. November 24, 1798   M. November 29, 1798
    Minister: William Creath   Surety: Matthew Turner

HUTCHESON, Richard, Jr.   Wilmouth Turner
    M.B. October 11, 1804   Surety: Jacob Shelor
    Minister: William Creath
    Note: Richard, Jr., son of John Hutcheson

HUTCHESON, Samuel   Hannah C. Brame
    M.B. October 18, 1796   M. October 27, 1796
    Minister: Charles Ogburn   Surety: William Phillips
    Consent: James Brame, guardian of Hannah

HUTCHESON, William   Amy W. Brown
    M.B. December 13, 1790   Surety: Thomas Brown

HYDE, John   Anne Walton
    M.B. November 16, 1786   M. December 21, 1786
    Minister: Henry Lester   Surety: Edward Walton
    Note: John, son of John Hyde, Senr.

INGE, Richard   Sarah Johnson
    M.B. November 7, 1785   November 9, 1785
    Minister: Devereaux Jarrott   Surety: William Davis

INGRAM, John   Sarah Collier
    M.B. June 7, 1773   Surety: Charles Hutcheson

INGRAM, Samuel   Martha Vaughan
    M.B. September 25, 1792   M. October 4, 1792
    Minister: William Creath   Surety: William Green

ISHAM, Frederick   Frances Avory
    M.B. November 10, 1794   M. November 22, 1794
    Minister: William Creath   Surety: Harwood Rudd

IVEY, Frederick   Prissey Stewart
    M.B. December 14, 1795   M. December 29, 1795
    Minister: William Creath   Surety: William Willis

JACKSON, Beckley   Martha Brown
      M.B. June 12, 1809   Surety: William Hutcheson

JACKSON, Bins   Polly Turner
      M.B. April 23, 1803   Surety: Drury Turner
      Minister: William Creath

JACKSON, Burwell   Nancy Thompson
      M.B. November 19, 1803   Surety: Drury Turner

JACKSON, Fleming   Patty Power
      M.B. October 9, 1792   Surety: Sampson Power

JACKSON, Francis   Elizabeth Curtis
      M.B. May 2, 1807   M. May 16, 1807
      Minister: Charles Ogburn   Surety: Samuel Simmons

JACKSON, Jaral   Mary Garrott
      M.B. November 13, 1798   M. November 22, 1798
      Minister: William Creath   Surety: Cavel Jackson
      Consent: Thomas Garrott, father of Mary

JACKSON, Mark Lambert   Drucilla Rainey
      M.B. November 8, 1784   Surety: Francis Rainey

JACKSON, Mark L.   Leannah Basey Webb
      M.B. July 3, 1797   Surety: John Webb

JACKSON, Nathaniel   Nancy Turner
      M.B. December 24, 1804   Surety: William Baskervill
      Minister: William Creath

JACKSON, Reuben   Annis Ligon
      M.B. March 10, 1800   M. March 25, 1800
      Minister: William Richards   Surety: John Walker

JACKSON, Sally (Salle')   Celey Epperson
      M.B. October 2, 1802   M. October 7, 1802
      Minister: Baalam Ezell   Surety: Henry Jackson

JACKSON, William   Nancy Bugg
      M.B. September 11, 1807   Surety: John Bugg

JARROTT, Zachariah   Peggy M. Burton
      M.B. April 12, 1806   Surety: Jones Burton

JEFFRIES, Achilles   Elizabeth Smith
      M.B. September 14, 1772   Surety: Drury Smith
      Consent: Eli Smith, father of Elizabeth

JEFFRIES, Benjamin W.   Nancy Evans
      M.B. December 11, 1809   M. December 14, 1809
      Minister: William Richards   Surety: Matthew Baptist

JEFFRIES, James   Ann Hogan
    M.B. May 11, 1789   M. June 2, 1789
    Minister: John Williams   Surety: Lewis Toone

JEFFRIES, John L.   Rebecca Richards
    M.B. September 8, 1806   Surety: William Richards

JEFFRIES, Richard   Jane Whitehead
    M.B. July 1, 1783   Surety: Robert Smith

JEFFRIES, Richard   Prudence Russell
    M.B. June 19, 1797   M. June 22, 1797
    Minister: William Richards   Surety: Thomas Burnett

JEFFRIES, Swepson, Senr.   Isabell Goode
    M.B. February 8, 1789   Surety: Benjamin Pennington

JEFFRIES, Swepson, Jr.   Elizabeth Coleman
    M.B. March 6, 1788   Surety: William Baskervill
    Minister: Thomas Scott
    Consent: Swepson Jeffries, Sr., father of Swepson,
    Note: Elizabeth, daughter of Cluverius Coleman

JEFFRIES, Swepson, Jr.   Sarah Minor
    M.B. March 10, 1800   Surety: George Minor

JEFFRIES, Thomas   Mary Richeson
    M.B. February 26, 1798   M. February 28, 1798
    Minister: Edward Almand   Surety: James Harrison

JEFFRIES, William B.   Elizabeth Jeffries
    M.B. October 5, 1801   Surety: Richard Jeffries
    Minsiter: Edward Almand

JETER, Charles P.   Mary Phillips
    M.B. December 22, 1802   Surety: Williamson Patillo
    Consent: Dabney Phillips, Sr., father of Mary

JETER, William   Lucy Speed
    M.B. December 11, 1780   Surety: Dabney Phillips

JOHNSON, Allen   Polly Hutcheson
    M.B. November 12, 1792   M. November 13, 1792
    Minister: Aaron Brown   Surety: Chiles Hutcheson

JOHNSON, Archer   Nancy Durham
    M.B. May 14, 1804   M. May 25, 1804
    Minister: William Richards   Surety: James Williams

JOHNSON, Isaac   Rebecca Bowen
    M.B. January 30, 1802   Surety: Littleberry Bowen

JOHNSON, Jacob   Linchey Crowder
    M.B. February 5, 1795   M. February 7, 1795
    Minister: Charles Ogburn   Surety: Edmund Burnett
    Consent: John Crowder, father of Linchey

JOHNSON, James   Sally Russell
    M.B. February 28, 1786   Surety: John Tisdale

JOHNSON, James   Elizabeth Russell
    M.B. October 30, 1780   Surety: Jeremiah Crowder

JOHNSON, James   Sarah Pettus
    M.B. November 10, 1794   Surety: Thomas Pettus

JOHNSON, James   Patsy Reader
    M.B. January 14, 1799   M. January 31, 1799
    Minister: William Richards   Surety: Thomas Reader

JOHNSON, John   Elizabeth Harrison
    M.B. January 11, 1802   M. January 21, 1802
    Minister: William Richards Surety: Greenwood Harrison

JOHNSON, John   Betsy Green Marshall
    M.B. December 22, 1802   Surety: Jordan McKinney
    Consent: Richard Marshall, father of Betsy

JOHNSON, John   Parmelia Mayne
    M.B. December 10, 1804   M. December 11, 1804
    Minister: Edward Almand   Surety: Samuel Weatherford
    Consent: James Mayne, father of Parmelia
    Note: John Johnson of Charlotte County

JOHNSON, John   Martha Toone
    M.B. January 27, 1810   Surety: Thomas Johnson

JOHNSON, Michael   Sally Carter
    M.B. December 10, 1781   Surety: John Johnson

JOHNSON, Phillip   Polly Stainback
    M.B. January 24, 1794   Surety: Daniel Wilson
    Consent: Laura Stainback, mother of Polly
    Consent: William Johnson, father of Phillip

JOHNSON, William Whitehead, Jr.   Minor Parsons Scott
    M.B. July 29, 1793   M. August 27, 1793
    Minister: William Creath   Surety: Samuel Scott
    Consent: William Johnson, father of William

JOHNSTON, James   Sarah Cox
    M.B. September 12, 1796   Surety: James Johnson

JONES, Benjamin   Linne Pierce
    M.B. June 10, 1803   Surety: Richard Jones
    Consent: Lucy Pierce, mother of Linne

JONES, Benjamin   Jane S. Coleman
    M.B. December 12, 1808   Surety: William Coleman
    Note: Jane Swenson, daughter of James Coleman,
          deceased

JONES, Cleaton   Parthena Crew
    M.B. July 13, 1807   M. July 17, 1807
    Minister: William Richards   Surety: Ruel Allen

JONES, Daniel   Martha Hamlin
    M.B. March 31, 1792   Surety: Thomas Vaughan
    Note: Martha, daughter of Thomas Hamlin
    Note: Daniel, son of Captain Thomas Jones

JONES, Darling   Keziah Blacketter
    M.B. March 21, 1798   Surety: William Jones

JONES, Edward   Sarah Butler
    M.B. July 9, 1792   M. July 19, 1792
    Minister: James Read   Surety: Elijah Graves

JONES, Francis   Nancy Booth
    M.B. September 18, 1799   Surety: Harper Booth
    Consent: Thomas Booth, father of Nancy

JONES, Frederick   Nelly Brooks
    M.B. October 16, 1787   Surety: Jurdain Brooks
    Consent: Robert Brooks, father of Nelly

JONES, Major Harwood   Rachel Crenshaw
    M.B. October 20, 1809   M. October 24, 1809
    Minister: William Richards   Surety: G. H. Baskervill
    Consent: Thomas A. Jones, guardian of Rachel

JONES, James   Elizabeth Holmes
    M.B. December 20, 1790   Surety: Pennington Holmes

JONES, James   Nancy Robertson
    M.B. October 13, 1794   M. October 19, 1794
    Minister: William Creath   Surety: James Hudson

JONES, James   Ann Hurt
    M.B. March 13, 1804   M. April 19, 1804
    Minister: William Richards
                                 Surety: Philemon Hurt, Jr.

JONES, James B.   Jane J. Davis
    M.B. August 3, 1810   Surety: G. H. Baskervill

JONES, John   Judith Booth
    M.B. January 22, 1807   Surety: Harper Booth
    Minister: James Meacham

JONES, Joseph   Ann B. Rogers
    M.B. December 7, 1807   Surety: James Whitlow, Jr.

JONES, Peter   Sarah Jackson
    M.B. December 11, 1797   Surety: Jeremiah Clanch

JONES, Richard   Nancy Hamblin
    M.B. February 23, 1799   Surety: Daniel Jones
    Consent: Thomas Hamblin, father of Nancy

JONES, Robert   Mary Morgan
    M.B. December 14, 1795   M. December 24, 1795
    Minister: William Creath   Surety: Samuel Puryear

JONES, Robert   Elizabeth Guy
    M.B. August 8, 1809   Surety: Daniel Guy
    Consent: Lucy Guy, mother of Elizabeth

JONES, Robert   Betsy Ann Jackson
    M.B. December 8, 1810   Surety: Mark L. Jackson

JONES, Robert H.   Elizabeth Baskervill
    M.B. April 9, 1807   Surety: Robert Park
    Minister: Charles Ogburn

JONES, Samuel   Dosha Hailey
    M.B. March 9, 1789   Surety: Daniel Jones
    Note: Dosha, daughter of Thomas Hailey

JONES, Thomas   Nancy Winfield
    M.B. November 26, 1787   Surety: Joshua Winfield

JONES, Thomas A.   Mary Crenshaw
    M.B. December 18, 1799   Surety: James Jones

JONES, Tignal (Sr.)   Sarah Anderson
    M.B. November 16, 1767   Surety: Tignal Jones, Jr.
    Note: Sarah, daughter of Thomas Anderson

JONES, William   Susanna Clark
    M.B. December 26, 1792   M. December 27, 1792
    Minister: William Creath   Surety: John Hudson

JONES, William   Charity Jackson
    M.B. October 22, 1794   M. October 24, 1794
    Minister: William Creath   Surety: John M. Carter

JONES, William   Lucy Lockett
    M.B. December 14, 1801   M. December 15, 1801
    Minister: William Richards   Surety: James Wilson
    Note: Lucy, daughter of Abner Lockett

JONES, William   Patsy B. Rogers
    M.B. December 8, 1810   Surety: Joseph Jones

JONES, Willis   Polly Stone
    M.B. November 4, 1803   Surety: William Stone
    Minister: William Creath
    Note: Polly, daughter of William and Tabitha Stone

JORDAN, Miles   Harriett Pettus
    M.B. November 12, 1804   Surety: John Pettus
    Consent: William Pettus, brother and guardian of
              Harriett Pettus
    Minister: John Cameron

KEEN, Abraham   Margaret Tabb
    M.B. December 29, 1790   Surety: Edward L. Tabb

KEETON, John   Nancy Allgood
    M.B. May 5, 1792   Surety: William Westbrook
    Consent: Moses Allgood, father of Nancy
    Note: John, son of Joseph Keeton

KEETON, Joseph   Sarah Cheatham
    M.B. August 8, 1803   M. August 31, 1803
    Minister: Matthew Dance   Surety: Warner Keeton

KEETON, Joseph   Betsy Moore
    M.B. October 13, 1806   Surety: James Johnson

KEETON, Leonard   Polly Tucker
    M.B. November 10, 1794   M. November 22, 1794
    Minister: William Creath   Surety:Daniel Tucker

KEETON, Leonard   Mary Tucker
    M.B. March 9, 1801   Surety: Thomas Coley
    Minister: William Creath

KEETON, Thomas   Nancy Bing
    M.B. November 13, 1805   Surety: James Keeton

KEETON, Warner   Lucy Mason
    M.B. February 13, 1804   Surety: William Stone
    Minister: William Creath

KEETON, William   Elizabeth Bing
    M.B. November 12, 1798   M. November 20, 1798
    Minister: William Creath   Surety: Thomas Dance
    Consent: George Bing, father of Elizabeth

KELLEY, Francis   Delilah Crowder
    M.B. May 25, 1785   Surety: William Baskervill
    Consent: George Crowder, father of Delilah

KELLEY, Henry   Mary Roberts
    M.B. March 13, 1793   N. March 14, 1793
    Minister: John Loyd   Surety: William Nanney
    Note: Henry Kelley of Brunswick County

KELLY, Abner   Molly Lanier
    M.B. February 23, 1798   M. March 1, 1798
    Minister: Charles Ogburn   Surety: John Feagins
    Consent: Leonard Lanier, father of Molly

KELLY, John   Frances Crowder
    M.B. December 6, 1804   Surety: Charles Kelly

KENDRICK, James   Elizabeth Wright
    M.B. December 12, 1797   Surety: John Wright

KENNON, Erasmus   Anne Carter Nelson
    M.B. November 14, 1808   Surety: George Craighead
    Minister: George Micklejohn

KENNON, Richard   Elizabeth Beverley Munford
    M.B. May 16, 1780   Surety: William Randolph
    Consent: Robert Munford, father of Elizabeth
    Note: Richard Kennon of Chesterfield County

KIDD, James   Frances Robertson
    M.B. August 8, 1795   Surety: Mark Robertson

KIDD, William   Judy Carter
    M.B. October 8, 1781   Surety: Leman Williams

KING, Charles   Elizabeth C. Hutcheson
    M.B. December 16, 1809   Surety: John Poyner

KING, Henry   Sarah Taylor
    M.B. July 18, 1804   Surety: James Minge Thompson
    Note: Henry King of Brunswick County

KING, James   Sarah Morgan
    M.B. March 27, 1779   Surety: Reuben Morgan
    Note: Sarah, daughter of Reuben Morgan

KING, Capt. Miles   Frances Powell Burwell
    M.B. July 15, 1799   Surety: William Baskervill
    Consent: Ann Burwell, mother of Frances
    Minister: John Cameron
    Note: Rev. John S. Ravenscroft states that Captain
          Miles King is from Norfolk

KIRKLAND, George   Martha Johnson Stainback
    M.B. June 29, 1809   Surety: Phillip Johnson
    Minister: James Meacham   M. July 12, 1809

KIRKS, Charles   Mary Persize
    M.B. November 10, 1787   M. November 13, 1787
    Minister: Edward Almand   Surety: Joseph Moon

KIRKS, William   Ann Parham
    M.B. July 8, 1788   Surety: Lewis Parham

KIRKS, William   Jane Arnold
    M.B. January 26, 1790   Surety: James McCann
    Consent: Samuel Kirks, father of William

KNIGHT, William   Elizabeth Oliver
    M.B. October 16, 1799   Surety: Richard Oliver
    Minister: William Creath

LADD, Amos   Elizabeth Crowder
    M.B. October 15, 1792   M. October 16, 1792
    Minister: John Loyd   Surety: John Ladd, Jr.

LADD, John, Jr.   Jincy Cleaton
    M.B. December 12, 1798   Surety: Joseph Ladd
    Minister: Ebenezer Macgowan

LADD, Noble   Mary Rottenberry
    M.B. December 29, 1792   M. January 3, 1793
    Minister: John Loyd   Surety: John Ladd

LADD, Thomas, Jr.   Mary Crowder
    M.B. August 6, 1788   Surety: Josiah Floyd

LADD, William   Martha Gilliam
    M.B. February 8, 1787   Surety: Jacob Ladd

LADD, William   Faitha Pennington
    M.B. December 29, 1800   Surety: John T. Pennington
    Consent: Henry Pennington, father of Faitha

LAFFOON, Nathaniel   Polly Merryman
    M.B. December 18, 1804   Surety: John Nash

LAFFOON, Nathaniel   Mary Chambliss
    M.B. November 17, 1808   Surety: George Small

LAINE, Benjamin   Patsy M. Mayne
    M.B. November 10, 1800   M. November 20, 1800
    Minister: Edward Almand   Surety: Owen Lowry
    Consent: James Mayne, father of Patsy

LAMAY, Richard   Elizabeth Cook
    M.B. January 18, 1804   Surety: Herbert Cook

LAMBERT, Ezekiel   Biddy Roberts
    M.B. February __, 1804 *   Surety: Robert Roberts
    * Day of month not given on bond

LAMBERT, John   Jemima Jackson
    M.B. August 2, 1785   Surety: Joseph Lambert

LAMBERT, John   Elizabeth Gregory
    M.B. December 11, 1809   Surety: William Vaughan
    Consent: Richard Gregory, father of Elizabeth

LAMBERT, Julius   Jincy Brooks
    M.B. December 13, 1796   M. December 14, 1796
    Minister: John Loyd   Surety: John McKinney

LAMBERT, Thomas   Frances Watson
    M.B. April 18, 1797   Surety: Richard Stone

LAMBERT, William   Sarah Bottom
    M.B. May 31, 1800   M. May 1, 1800
    Minister: Ebenezer Macgowan   Surety: James Burton

LAMKIN, Cleophas   Mary Doggett
    M.B. December 19, 1785   M. December 23, 1785
    Minister: John Marshall   Surety: James Garner
    Consent: John and Mary Doggett, parents of Mary

LANGLEY, John   Lucy Young
    M.B. December 6, 1798   Surety: Allen Young

LANGLEY, Thomas   Joyce Bugg
    M.B. April 24, 1773   Surety: Samuel Hopkins

LANGLEY, Walter C.   Judith B. Young
    M.B. November 5, 1803   Surety: Jesse Dortch
    Consent: Allen Young, father of Judith

LANIER, Allen   Polly Davis
    M.B. November 21, 1791   Surety: Josiah Floyd
    Minister: John King
    Consent: Charles and Martha Floyd, parents of Polly

LANIER, Nicholas   Sarah Bugg
    M.B. March 23, 1796   M. April 2, 1796
    Minister: James Tolleson   Surety: John Nance

LANIER, William   Mary Garland Ballard
    M.B. September 4, 1794   Surety: James Bullock
    Consent: John Ballard, father of Mary Garland
    Note:James Bullock of Granville County, N. C.
    Note: John Ballard (Sr.) names granddaughter Mary
          Garland Ballard in will

LEACH, James, Jr.   Patsy Gregory
    M.B. January 18, 1802   Surety: Francis Gregory
    Consent: Roger Gregory, Sr., father of Patsy

LEE, Amos   Elizabeth Thompson
    M.B. November 13, 1809   M. December 28, 1809
    Minister: William Richards
                            Surety: Margarian Thompson

LEE, Jesse   Elizabeth Northington
    M.B. December 3, 1803   Surety: Samuel Butler

LEIGH, Anselm   Sally Greenwood
    M.B. January 20, 1790   Surety: Walter Leigh
    Consent: Thomas Greenwood, father of Sally
    Note: Anselm and Walter of Richmond County, Ga.

LEIGH, Walter   Patty Holmes
    M.B. December 1, 1784   Surety: Samuel Holmes
    Note: Patty (Martha) Holmes, daughter of Samuel
          Holmes
    Note: Walter Leigh moved to Richmond County, Ga.

LETT, Francis   Elizabeth Thompson
    M.B. September 21, 1797   Surety: James Lett

LETT, Hardaway   Mary Burton
    M.B. September 1, 1806   Surety: Pennington Lett

LETT, Joseph, Jr.   Polly Jeffries Burnett
    M.B. January 28, 1804   Surety: Matthew H. Davis
    Consent: Thomas Burnett, father of Polly

LETT, Pennington   Frances Pennington
    M.B. February 14, 1810   Surety: John T. Pennington
    Consent: Josiah Floyd, guardian of Frances

LETT, Robert   Suckey Burrus Lett
    M.B. April 17, 1794   M. April 18, 1794
    Minister: John Loyd   Surety: William Parrish

LEWIS, Abraham   Elizabeth Clark
    M.B. October 8, 1804   Surety: James Parham

LEWIS, Abraham   Louisa Averett
    M.B. February 11, 1805   M. February 21, 1805
    Minister William Richards
                            Surety: C. Granderson Feild

LEWIS, Charles   Mary Anderson
    M.B. November 8, 1779   Surety: Howell Taylor
    Consent: Thomas Anderson (Sr.), father of Mary

LEWIS, Edward   Elizabeth Clark
    M.B. August 10, 1807   Surety: Overton Wiles

LEWIS, Francis   Elizabeth Hester
    M.B. April 27, 1786   M. April 30, 1786
    Minister: Henry Lester   Surety: Henry Sandifer
    Consent: William Baker, guardian of Elizabeth
    Note: Elizabeth, daughter of Abraham Hester, deceased

LEWIS, James   Susannah Anderson
    M.B. June 25, 1774   Surety: Thomas Anderson
    Note: Susannah, daughter of Thomas Anderson (Sr.)

LEWIS, Robert   Ann Bugg
    M.B. November 10, 1788   Surety: Samuel Bugg
    Minister: John Cameron
    Note: Robert Lewis of Granville County, N. C.

LEWIS, Robert   Elizabeth Jones
    M.B. February 25, 1794   Surety: Asa Thomas
    Consent: Tignal Jones, father of Elizabeth

LEWIS, Robert   Nancy Willis
    M.B. August 22, 1799   Surety:Edward Willis
    Consent: Edward Lewis, father of Robert
    Consent: William Willis, father of Nancy

LEWIS, Robert   Charlotte Butler
    M.B. January 8, 1810   Surety: Jones Allen

LEWIS, Thomas   Elizabeth Birtchett
    M.B. March 22, 1806   Surety: John Dortch
    Minister: Thomas Hardie

LIGON, James   Hannah Christopher
    M.B. October 11, 1796   M. November 24, 1796
    Minister: William Richards   Surety: John Ligon

LIGON, James   Anne Gregory
    M.B. November 14, 1798   Surety: James Reamy
    Minister: William Richards   M. November 22, 1798

LIPFORD, John   Lettice Jones
    M.B. December 3, 1796   Surety: Buckner Whittemore

LISK, William   Dicy Eastham
    M.B. December 21, 1803   Surety: Richard Crowder

LOCKETT, Francis   Martha Goode Marshall
    M.B. March 8, 1802   Surety: Valentine McCutcheon
    Consent: William Marshall, father of Martha
    Note: Francis, son of Abner and Ann Lockett

LOCKETT, Royall   Prudence Clay
    M.B. August 20, 1789   Surety: James Elam
    Consent: Charles and Phebe Clay, parents of
              Prudence

LOLLIS, John   Aggy Spurlock, Jr.
    M.B. April 5, 1786   Surety: John Hatsell

LONNON, Henry   Mary Elam
    M.B. December 13, 1803   M. December 15, 1803
    Minister: Edward Almand   Surety: Phillip Ryan

LOVE, William   Susanna Brame
    M.B. May 6, 1803   Surety: Ingram Roffe
    Consent: James Brame, guardian of Susanna
    Note: Susanna, daughter of Thomas Brame

LUCAS, Frederick   Martha Baskervill
    M.B. October 27, 1779   Surety: William Baskervill
    Note: Martha, daughter of George Baskervill

LUCAS, George   Patty Arnold
    M.B. March 21, 1770   Surety: James Arnold
    Note: Martha, (Patty), daughter of James Arnold, Sr.
          and Martha Arnold

LUCAS, Dr. John R.   Hannah H. Brown
    M.B. April 26, 1806   Surety: John Dortch
    Consent: R. Watson, guardian of Hannah
    Minister: James Meacham
    Note: Hannah Brown of Brunswick County

LUMPKIN, Anthony   Polly Yancey
    M.B. November 14, 1808   Surety: Charles Yancey

LUMSDON, John   Elizabeth Eastland
    M.B. February 8, 1788   M. February 9, 1788
    Minister: Edward Almand   Surety: Robert White

82

LUNSFORD, Moses   Mary Fox
    M.B. January 28, 1796   Surety: John McKenny
    Minister: John Loyd
    Consent: Richard Fox, father of Mary

McCARTER, James   Liza Bowen
    M.B. December 3, 1804   Surety: James Bowen

McCARTER, Thomas   Caty Bowen
    M.B. June 23, 1803   Surety: James Bowen
    Minister: William Creath

McCUTCHEON, Charles   Prudence Evans
    M.B. December 11, 1797   Surety: Richard Jeffries
    Minister: Edward Almand   M. December 14, 1797

McCUTCHEON, Valentine   Anna Hester
    M.B. March 10, 1800   M. March 18, 1800
    Minister: William Richards   Surety: Richard Brown

McDANIEL, William   Rody Mason
    M.B. August 11, 1795   M. August 13, 1795
    Minister: Charles Ogburn   Surety: Ezekiel Redding

MacGOWAN, Ebenezer   Frances Baugh
    M.B. July 29, 1797   Surety: James Baugh
    Note: Frances, daughter of James and Agnes Baugh

McKINNEY, John   Elizabeth Douglas
    M.B. December 24, 1792   M. December 27, 1792
    Minister: John Loyd   Surety: David Thomas
    Consent: S. Douglas, father of Elizabeth

McKINNEY, Munford   Patsy Morgan
    M.B. December 10, 1789   M. December 17, 1789
    Minister: John Phaup   Surety: John Morgan

McKINNEY, Willis   Nancy Glover
    M.B. February 25, 1801   M. February 26, 1801
    Minister: Ebenezer Macgowan   Surety: William Blanton

McLIN, Thomas   Delilah Evans
    M.B. December 23, 1794   M. December 24, 1794
    Minister: John Loyd   Surety: John Guy

McLIN, William   Anne Venable
    M.B. April __, 1801 *   Surety: James McLin
    Note: William McLin of Greensville County
    * Day of month not given on bond

McQUIE, William   Sarah Brook
    M.B. January 11, 1785   Surety: Burwell Russell

MABRY, Stephen   Tabitha Nance
    M.B. April 19, 1775   Surety: John Cook
    Consent: Isham Nance, brother of Tabitha

MALLETT, Thomas   Betsy H. Allgood
    M.B. February __, 1804 *   Surety: George Allgood
    Minister: William Creath
    * Day of month not legible on bond

MALONE, Drury   Penelope Taylor
    M.B. June 14, 1774   Surety: Lewis Parham

MALONE, Frederick   Susannah Bilbo
    M.B. May 24, 1774   Surety: John Bilbo

MALONE, Frederick   Judith Puckett
    M.B. May 19, 1779   Surety: John Puckett
    Note: John Puckett of North Carolina, place not stated

MALONE, George   Sarah Fowlkes
    M.B. October 23, 1804   M. October 25, 1804
    Minister: William Richards   Surety: Gabriel Fowlkes

MALONE, Isaac   Ann C. Courtney
    M.B. September 22, 1790   M. September 23, 1790
    Minister: John King   Surety: Josiah Floyd

MALONE, Isaac   * Lucy Sawsberry
    M.B. March 24, 1795   Surety: Joseph Walker
    Minister: John Loyd
    * Probably "Saulsberry"

MALONE, Nathaniel   Elizabeth Evans
    M.B. May 31, 1777   Surety: Stephen Mabry
    Consent: Stephen Evans, father of Elizabeth

MANNING, Benjamin   Fanny Guy
    M.B. May 5, 1796   Surety: Earbe Chavous
    Minister: John Loyd   M. May 8, 1796

MARABLE, John   Lucy R. Billups
    M.B. December 12, 1791   M. December 13, 1791
    Minister: John Williams   Surety: John Billups

MARABLE, William   Frances Christopher
    M.B. December 1, 1801   M. December 5, 1801
    Minister: William Richards   Surety: Jesse Hord

MARSHALL, Burnett   Lucy Wilson
    M.B. October 13, 1803   Surety: Frederick Watkins
    Consent: James Wilson, guardian of Lucy

MARSHALL, Dennis   Frances Harper
    M.B. August 27, 1792   Surety: John Harper
    Note: Dennis, son of Samuel and Cassandra (Alfriend)
        Marshall

MARSHALL, Francis   Jane Hester
    M.B. November 7, 1803   Surety: Daniel Johnson
    Minister: William Creath
    Consent: Samuel Hester, father of Jane

MARSHALL, Isaac   Sally Finn
    M.B. May 23, 1795   M. May 26, 1795
    Minister: John Loyd   Surety: David Pennington

MARSHALL, Josiah   Elizabeth Winn
    M.B. February 17, 1802   M. March 3, 1802
    Minister: William Richards   Surety: Banister Winn

MARSHALL, Thomas   Elizabeth L. Baptist
    M.B. March 1, 1802   Surety: John G. Baptist
    Minister: William Creath
    Consent: William Glanvil Baptist, father of Eliza-
        beth Baptist

MARSHALL, William   Rebeccah Evans
    M.B. December 17, 1803   Surety: Matthew Evans

MARTIN, James   Dolly Ridley
    M.B. June 8, 1789   Surety: Samuel Puryear

MARTIN, James   Margaret Allen
    M.B. March 12, 1800   Surety: John Puryear, Jr.
    Minister: William Creath

MARTIN, John   Cary Crowder
    M.B. May 30, 1797   M. June 1, 1797
    Minister: William Richards
                               Surety: Philemon Hurt, Jr.

MARTIN, John   Elizabeth Coppedge
    M.B. April 3, 1799   M. April 4, 1799
    Minister: Ebenezer Macgowan
                               Surety: Charles Coppedge

MARTIN, Oliver   Elizabeth Mallett
    M.B. March 13, 1799   M. March 21, 1799
    Minister: William Creath   Surety: Richard M. Allen

MARTIN, Warner   Martha Bailey
    M.B. October 6, 1783   Surety: Benjamin Ferrell
    Consent: William Bailey, father of Martha

MASON, Jordan   Agnes Walker
    M.B. October 10, 1808   Surety: Allen Walker
    Note: Agnes, daughter of Richard and Lucy Walker

MASON, Robert   Martha Johnson
    M.B. March 31, 1797   M. April 3, 1797
    Minister: Charles Ogburn   Surety: John Edwards
    Consent: Jincy Hawkins, mother of Patsy (Martha)

MASON, William   Susanna Campbell
    M.B. January 14, 1795   M. January 22, 1795
    Minister: John Loyd   Surety: Benjamin Fargeson, Jr.

MASON, William W.   Nancy Crenshaw
    M.B. September 9, 1805   M. September 13, 1805
    Minister: Matthew Dance   Surety: G. H. Baskervill

MASSEY, Peter   Hannah Wells
    M.B. March 11, 1802   Surety: William Garrott
    Minister: William Creath

MASSEY, Thomas   Peggy Barry
    M.B. April 24, 1799   Surety: James Johnson

MATTHEWS, Enos   Liddy Overby
    M.B. September 17, 1788   Surety: Richard Thompson
    Minister: Thomas Scott

MATTHEWS, John   Martha Wingfield Jordan
    M.B. December 18, 1799   M. December 24, 1799
    Minister: James Meacham   Surety: Wilkins Ogburn
    Consent: Mary Jordan, mother of Martha
    Note: John Matthews of Brunswick County

MATTHEWS, Thomas   Betsy Wilkerson
    M.B. March 22, 1809   Surety: John Rainey

MAYES, Bozeman   Mary Neal
    M.B. November 10, 1783   M. November 13, 1783
                                 Surety: William Hundley
    Consent: William Neal, father of Mary

MAYES, John   Elizabeth Hamblin
    M.B. January 7, 1789   Surety: John Wynne

MAYES, William   Lucretia Cox
    M.B. December 26, 1806   M. December 29, 1806
    Minister: William Richards   Surety: Miles Hall

MAYNARD, Wagstaff   Fanny Hord
    M.B. December 10, 1792   Surety: James Hord
    Note: Fanny, daughter of Thomas Hord

MAYNE, James   Sarah Tibbs
    M.B. March 8, 1779   Surety: William Tibbs

MAYO, Cuffey   Celey Stewart
    M.B. April 2, 1802   Surety: Daniel Mayo

MAYO, Hutchins   Sally Stewart
    M.B. February 10, 1806   Surety: Daniel Mayo
    Consent: Betsy Stewart, mother of Sally

MAYO, Pompy   Nancy Marks
    M.B. December 17, 1801   Surety: Minge Mayo

MEALER, Nicholas   Tabitha Ragsdale
    M.B. July 12, 1802   M. August 5, 1802
    Minister: William Richards   Surety: James Wilson

MEALER, Phillip   Patty Jones
    M.B. May 14, 1781   Surety: Jesse Saunders
    Consent: Thomas Jones, father of Patty

MEALER, William   Nancy Humphries
    M.B. September 11, 1775   Surety: John Humphries

MEALER, William   Elizabeth P. Puryear
    M.B. November 9, 1807   Surety: Thomas Lewis

MEDLEY, Bartholomew   Sally Holloway
    M.B. December 23, 1797   Surety: Benjamin Fargeson

MEDLEY, Joseph   Elanner White
    M.B. January 10, 1807   M. January 11, 1807
    Minister: William Richards   Surety: John Dortch

MEREDITH, Joseph N.   Mary Baptist
    M.B. May 12, 1800   Surety: G. H. Baskervill
    Minister: William Creath

MERRITT, Thomas *   Elizabeth Suggett
    M.B. December 14, 1785   Surety: Pennington Holmes
    Consent: Edgecomb Suggett, father of Elizabeth
    * Other records give name as Thomas Marriott

MERRYMAN, Epps   Amey Kirks
    M.B. January 26, 1790   Surety: James McCann

MERRYMAN, Epps   Elizabeth Thomerson
    M.B. January 5, 1803   Surety: William Thomerson

MERRYMAN, Isham   Lucretia Turner
    M.B. April 4, 1787   Surety: Abram Merryman

MILLER, Henry   Elizabeth Smith
    M.B. June 17, 1800   Surety: Zachariah Curtis

MILLS, Charles   Jincy Baker
    M.B. December 9, 1799   M. December 19, 1799
    Minister: Matthew Dance   Surety: George Baker

MILLS, John   Susanna Pool
    M.B. November 22, 1808   Surety: Robert Greenwood

MIMMS, John   Wilmouth Jones
    Minister: William Creath   * January __, 1788
    * Day of month not given

MIMMS, Thomas   Elizabeth Noel
    M.B. May 5, 1802   Surety: George Meanly

MITCHELL, Benjamin   Mary Stone
    M.B. December 14, 1795   Surety: William Stone

MITCHELL, Gideon   Sally Wagstaff
    M.B. February 7, 1804   M. February 8, 1804
    Minister: William Richards   Surety: Allen Wagstaff

MITCHELL, Ishmael   Elizabeth Nance
    M.B. January 6, 1808   Surety: Isham Nance, Jr.

MITCHELL, Reuben   Ann Pennington
    M.B. April 2, 1783   Surety: Edward Pennington

MITCHELL, Thomas   * ____ Malone
    M.B. August 3, 1785   Surety: John Burton
    * Marriage bond mutilated and name torn

MITCHELL, Thomas   Fanny Pully
    M.B. October 31, 1810   Surety: William Daly

MITCHELL, William   Elizabeth Warren
    M.B. July 22, 1786   Surety: Richard Stone
    Consent: Thomas Marriott, Sr., guardian of Elizabeth
    Note: Richard Stone of Brunswick County

MIZE, Henry   Elizabeth Yeargen
    M.B. January 12, 1807   Surety: John Mize
    Note: Henry Mize of Brunswick County

MIZE, John   Lemenda Lambert
    M.B. March 24, 1795   M. March 25, 1795
    Minister: John Loyd   Surety: Thomas Lambert

MIZE, John   Nancy Yeargen
    M.B. December 30, 1805   Surety: Jerry Mize

MIZE, Randolph   Martha Matthews
    M.B. April 28, 1798   M. May 3, 1798
    Minister: Ebenezer Macgowan   Surety: Hudson Nipper

MONDAY, Jesse   Judith Naish
    M.B. November 13, 1792   Surety: Moore Comer
    Note: Moore Comer of Halifax County

MONROE, John   Margaret Culbreath
    M.B. March 10, 1789   Surety: Thomas Culbreath

MONTAGUE, Mickelborough   Nancy Vaughan
    M.B. July 30, 1798   M. August 2, 1798
    Minister: William Creath   Surety: Reuben Vaughan
    Note: Nancy (Ann Carter) Vaughan, daughter of Reuben
        and Elizabeth (Ingram) Vaughan

MONTGOMERY, Richard P.   Sarah Hudson
    M.B. January 30, 1804   M. February 2, 1804
    Minister: Matthew Dance   Surety: Richard Hudson

MOODY, Arthur   Mary Hester
    M.B. December 13, 1796   M. December 15, 1796
    Minister: William Richards   Surety: James Palmer
    Consent: James Hester, father of Mary

MOODY, Francis   Patsy Vaughan
    M.B. September 14, 1789   Surety: William Moody
    Consent: Henry Moody, father of Francis
    Consent: Reuben Vaughan, father of Patsy (Martha)
    Minister: Thomas Scott
    Note: Martha Vaughan, daughter of Reuben and
        Elizabeth Ingram Vaughan

MOODY, Francis   Anna Hester
    M.B. December 26, 1805   Surety: Harwood Jones
    Minister: Thomas Hardie
    Consent: James Hester, father of Anna

MOODY, Henry   Polly Moody
    M.B. June 20, 1793   M. June 29, 1793
    Minister: William Creath   Surety: Robert Hester
    Consent: Arthur Moody, father of Polly

MOON, Joseph   Jane Johnson
    M.B. January 24, 1787   Surety: Isaac Johnson

MOORE, Feild   Sarah Lidderdal
    M.B. November 26, 1774   Surety: Thomas Moore
    Consent: Thomas Anderson, guardian of Sarah

MOORE, George   Elizabeth Moody
     M.B. July 14, 1788   M. July 24, 1788
     Minister: John Williams   Surety: Thomas Moore

MOORE, John   Hannah Hutcheson
     M.B. August 11, 1801   Surety: Charles Hutcheson
     Minister: William Creath

MOORE, Philip B.   Phebe Elam
     M.B. December __ , 1789 *   M. December 24, 1789
     Minister: John Williams   Surety: Peter Elam
     * Day of month not given on bond - Return says 24th

MOORE, Robert   Nancy Harrison
     M.B. July 21, 1796   Surety: John Ogburn
     Minister: Charles Ogburn

MOORE, Starling   Huldy Ladd
     M.B. December 27, 1791   M. December 29, 1791
     Minister: John Loyd   Surety: William Drumwright

MOORE, Warner   Betsy Edwards Northington
     M.B. May 6, 1805   Surety: Robert Moore
     Consent: Jabez Northington, father of Betsy

MOORE, William, Jr.   Jane Williams
     M.B. November 8, 1787   Surety: William Moore, Senr.
     Consent: Elizabeth Williams, mother of Jane

MORGAN, Benjamin   Mary Bilbo
     M.B. December 19, 1785   M. December 22, 1785
     Minister: John King   Surety: Frederick Rainey
     Consent: James Bilbo, father of Mary

MORGAN, John   Agnes Bilbo
     M.B. August 24, 1779   Surety: Joseph Bilbo
     Consent: James Bilbo, father of Agnes

MORGAN, John   Mary Pool
     M.B. February 17, 1790   Surety: Phil Morgan

MORGAN, John   Lucy Royster
     M.B. March 9, 1801   M. March 26, 1801
     Minister: William Richards   Surety: John Pritchett

MORGAN, John   Sarah Chamberlain
     M.B. _____ , 1803 *   M. April   , 1803
     Minister: William Creath   Surety: Nathaniel Moss
     * Bond mutilated with only year date legible
     Note: Minister's return says April 1803

90

MORGAN, John, Jr.   Nancy Cole
     M.B. March 14, 1789   Surety: Philip Morgan, Sr.

MORGAN, Philip   Patty Puckett
     M.B. October 13, 1784   Surety: Frederick Rainey

MORGAN, Starling   Celia Loyd
     M.B. August 7, 1797   M. August 10, 1797
     Minister: Charles Ogburn   Surety: John Loyd

MORGAN, Starling   Martha Howard
     M.B. October ___, 1802*   Surety: Stephen Roberts
     * Bond torn and day of month not legible

MORRIS, Daniel   Nancy Saunders
     M.B. December 15, 1807   Surety: John Feagins
     Consent: John Saunders, Sr., father of Nancy

MORRIS, Edward   Prudence Finn
     M.B. February 8, 1799   M. February 11, 1799
     Minister: William Creath   Surety: Nicholas Lanier

MORRIS, Henry   Lucy Drumwright
     M.B. December 15, 1807   Surety: William Drumwright

MORRIS, Jesse   Sally Williams Drumwright
     M.B. January 26, 1804   Surety: William Drumwright
     Consent: William Drumwright, father of Sally
     Minister: William Creath

MOSS, John   Rebecca Cox
     M.B. December 11, 1809   Surety: Charles Cox
     Minister: James Meacham   M. December 21, 1809

MOSS, Meredith   Nancy Osling
     M.B. May 21, 1792   M. May 31, 1792
     Minister: John Loyd   Surety: Samuel Oslin
     Consent: Jesse Osling, father of Nancy
     Note: Meredith Moss of Brunswick County

MOSS, Nathaniel   Helina Dortch
     M.B. October 8, 1777   Surety: Labon Wright

MOSS, Nathaniel   Martha Speed
     M.B. April 19, 1794   M. April 25, 1794
     Minister: John Loyd   Surety: Lewis Dortch

MOSS, Ray   Jane Coleman
     M.B. March 16, 1782   Surety: William Coleman
     Consent: Richard Coleman, relation not stated

MOSS, William   Sarah Stainback
    M.B. December 9, 1805   Surety: James Stainback
    Consent: Susie Stainback, mother of Sarah

MOSS, William   Mary Robinson
    M.B. October 12, 1809   M. October 13, 1809
    Minister: James Meacham   Surety: Henry Royall

MULLINS, Matthew   Elizabeth Crowder
    M.B. September 14, 1795   M. September 22, 1795
    Minister: William Richards   Surety: James Hudson

MULLINS, Valentine   Patsy Grigg
    M.B. November 10, 1794   M. November 13, 1794
    Minister: William Richards   Surety: James Hudson

MURPHEY, William   Elizabeth Eppes
    M.B. May 8, 1779   Surety: Isham Eppes

MUSTIAN, Jeffrey   Elizabeth Stegall
    M.B. February 5, 1787   Surety: James Chambliss

NANCE, Daniel   Sarah Russell
    M.B. March 13, 1780   Surety: James Standley

NANCE, Isham, Jr.   Nancy Rainey
    M.B. August 8, 1803   M. August 11, 1803
    Minister: Matthew Dance   Surety: Thomas Nance

NANCE, John   Frances Bugg
    M.B. April 10, 1786   Surety: Robert Nance
    Consent: John Bugg, father of Frances

NANCE, John   Frances Winn
    M.B. March 17, 1795   M. March 19, 1795
    Minister: John Loyd   Surety: John Thomas

NANCE, Robert   Fatha Pennington
    M.B. January 14, 1790   Surety: William Drumwright
    Consent: James Pennington, father of Fatha

NANCE, Thomas   Elizabeth Cleaton
    M.B. December 20, 1791   M. December 22, 1791
    Minister: John Loyd   Surety: Thomas Cleaton

NANCE, Thomas   Elizabeth Giles
    M.B. October 4, 1795   M. October 28, 1795
    Minister: John Loyd   Surety: John Cleaton

NANCE, Thomas   Sally Malone
    M.B. January 10, 1810   Surety: Thomas Cleaton

NANCE, William   Patsy Williams
    M.B. February 4, 1800   M. February 6, 1800
    Minister: Ebenezer Macgowan   Surety: Lewis Williams

NANCE, Wyatt   Polly Cook
    M.B. January 9, 1794   Surety: John Cook

NANNEY, Hewbery *   Patsy Roberts
    M.B. January 12, 1792   M. January 13, 1792
    Minister: John Loyd   Surety: John Fowler
    Consent: William Roberts, father of Patsy
    * Name written also as Huberry, Hugh Berry

NANNEY, Roberts   Sarah Morgan
    M.B. July 30, 1804   Surety: Starling Morgan
    Consent: Benjamin Morgan, father of Sarah

NANNEY, William   Frances King
    M.B. May 5, 1806   Surety: Hughberry Nanney
    Consent: Lewis King, father of Frances

NAISH, Abraham *   Polly Carter
    M.B. November 14, 1796   Surety: William Naish
    Minister: William Creath
    * Name written also as Nash

NASH, James   Sukey Pennington
    M.B. December 23, 1786   Sur: John George Pennington

NASH, John   Betsy Chambers
    M.B. December 16, 1795   M. December 17, 1795
    Minister: John Loyd   Surety: Williamson Patillo

NASH, Wiley   Anne Pennington
    M.B. January 5, 1807   Surety: John Harper

NASH, William   Leliah Hutt
    M.B. October 12, 1801   Surety: Thomas Hutt
    Minister: William Creath

NEAL, Edward   Sally Green
    M.B. December 8, 1806   M. December 17, 1806
    Minister: James Meacham   Surety: James T. Hayes
    Note: Edward, son of Francis Moore Neal
    Note: Sally, daughter of Matthew Green

NEAL, John   Clarissa Poindexter
    M.B. January 9, 1775   Surety: Moses Overton
    Note: Clarissa, daughter of Phillip Poindexter, Sr.

NEAL, Reaves   Elizabeth Worsham
    M.B. October 8, 1792   Surety: William Neal
    Minister: James Read

NEAL, Thomas   Elizabeth Brown
    M.B. January 1, 1787   Surety: Thomas Brown
    Note: Thomas, son of William Neal, Sr.

NEAL, Thomas   Elizabeth C. Coleman
    M.B. October 8, 1804   Surety: William Coleman
    Minister: James Meacham   M. October 23, 1804
    Note: Thomas, son of Francis Moore Neal
    Note: Elizabeth, daughter of James Coleman, deceased

NEBLETT, Sterling   Ann Daly
    M.B. October 4, 1798   M. October 8, 1798
    Minister: Charles Ogburn   Surety: Charles Ogburn
    Consent: Josiah Daly, father of Ann

NELSON, Norborne T.   Lucy Nelson
    M.B. April 8, 1805   M. April 15, 1805
    Minister: Alexander Hay   Surety: Henry Young

NETHERY, Thomas   Ann Baker
    M.B. January 27, 1789   Surety: George Baker
    Minister: Thomas Scott

NEWSOM, Robert   Martha Ruffin
    M.B. October 2, 1772   Surety: Francis Ruffin
    Consent: John Ruffin, father of Martha

NEWTON, James   Elizabeth Newton
    M.B. March 14, 1803   Surety: Robert Newton

NEWTON, Robert   Mary Read
    M.B. September 8, 1788   Surety: Elijah Graves

NICHOLSON, Starling   Elizabeth Moore
    M.B. July 5, 1802   Surety: Lewis Nicholson

NICHOLSON, William   Martha Hardy, Widow
    M.B. November 19, 1786   Sur: Richard Swepson, Senr.

NIPPER, Hutson   Frances Vaughan
    M.B. November 16, 1792   M. November 22, 1792
    Minister: John Loyd   Surety: Ambrose Vaughan

NIPPER, Pace   Rody Vaughan
    M.B. October 23, 1793   M. October 24, 1793
    Minister: John Loyd   Surety: Hudson Nipper

NORMENT, James   Jane Jeffries
    M.B. June 28, 1793   M. June 30, 1793
    Minister: John Williams   Surety: Richard Jeffries

NORMENT, Thomas   Ann Jeffries
    M.B. February 14, 1785   M. March 23, 1785
    Minister: John Marshall   Surety: John Jeffries

NORTHCROSS, William Renn   Frances Hatsell
    M.B. March 4, 1786   Surety: John McCarter

NORTHINGTON, David   Martha Crowder
    M.B. August 13, 1804   M. September 6, 1804
    Minister: James Watkins   Surety: Peter Crowder

NOWELL, Allen   Elizabeth Stewart
    M.B. July 14, 1800   Surety: Frederick Nowell

NOWELL, John   Elizabeth Chamberlain
    M.B. March 22, 1785   Surety: John Hamner
    Consent: Thomas Chamberlain, father of Elizabeth

NOWELL, Thomas   Sally Fox
    M.B. October 12, 1790   M. October 14, 1790
    Minister: John King   Surety: Thomas Roberts

O'BRIANT, John   Patsy Moss
    M.B. December 14, 1795   Surety: William Moore

OGBURN, Matthew   Sarah Daly
    M.B. February 15, 1792   M. February 16, 1792
    Minister: John Loyd   Surety: Charles Ogburn
    Consent: Josiah Daly, father of Sarah

OLIVER, Asa   Sarah Wray
    M.B. December 1, 1772   Surety: John Oliver

OLIVER, James W.   Elizabeth Green
    M.B. March 2, 1799   M. March 16, 1799
    Minister: William Creath   Surety: Abraham Green
    Note: James Wray Oliver, son of Asa and Sarah (Wray)
        Oliver

OLIVER, John   Elizabeth Bailey
    M.B. December 8, 1794   M. December 24, 1794
    Minister: Charles Ogburn   Surety: William Durham

OLIVER, Richard   Elizabeth Jeffries
    M.B. December 12, 1803   Surety: William Bilbo

OLIVER, Robert   Martha Moss
    M.B. December __, 1805 *   M. December 18, 1805
    Minister: James Meacham   Surety: Henry Coleman
    * Day of month not legible on bond - Return says 18th

ORGAN, Thomas   Sarah Lucas
    M.B. November 11, 1805   Surety: John Dortch

OSBORN, Jones   Nancy Fowlkes
    M.B. June 12, 1797   Surety: Edward Elam

OSLIN, Isaac   Ann Pennington
    M.B. March 1, 1800   Surety: David Pennington

OSLIN, Samuel   Martha Bugg
    M.B. March 7, 1789   Surety: John Bugg

OVERBY, Jechonias   Jane Greenwood
    M.B. January 11, 1796   Hume R. Feild
    Minister: William Creath

OVERBY, John   Elizabeth Childress
    M.B. June 11, 1804   Surety: William Overby
    Consent: Jincy Childress, mother of Elizabeth

OVERBY, William   Susannah Yancey
    M.B. June 11, 1804   Surety: Howell Graves

OVERTON, John   Susannah Christopher
    M.B. January 10, 1772   Surety: William Christopher
    Note: Susannah, daughter of David Christopher

OVERTON, John   Martha Elizabeth Ballard
    M.B. November 10, 1806   M. November 12, 1806
    Minister: Charles Ogburn   Surety: Francis Ballard

OVERTON, Thomas   Martha Toone
    M.B. April 13, 1795   M. April 16, 1795
    Minister: Edward Almand   Surety: Edward Hogan

OVERTON, William S.   Mary Baskervill
    M.B. December 10, 1799   Surety: E. Baskervill
    Minister: William Creath

OWEN, Sherwood   Sally Harris
    M.B. November 7, 1796   M. November 8, 1796
    Minister: Edward Almand   Surety: James Harris
    Note: Sally, daughter of James Harris
    Note: Sherwood Owen of Halifax County

PALMER, Amasa   Sally Davis
    M.B. March 2, 1774   Surety: William Davis

PALMER, Amasa   Judith Hendrick
    M.B. December 13, 1800   Surety: Christopher Haskins

PALMER, James   Martha Hester
    M.B. May 9, 1791   Surety: William Durham Watkins

PALMER, William   Elizabeth Lewis
    M.B. October 12, 1772   Surety: Edward Lewis

PARHAM, Lewis   Betsy Baird, Spinster
    M.B. May 22, 1769   Surety: John Tabb

PARRISH, Jesse   Elizabeth Hutcheson
    M.B. June 27, 1810   Surety: John Ingram

PARRISH, William   Frances Lett
    M.B. December 30, 1786   Surety: Isaac Adams

PARRISH, William   * Milla Tudor
    M.B. December 9, 1801   Surety: William Roberts
    * Camilla Tudor

PARRISH, William   Martha Rudd
    M.B. November 19, 1807   M. November 21, 1807
    Minister: Richard Dabbs   Surety: Augustine Smith

PATRICK, John   Sarah Kendrick
    M.B. September 29, 1779   Surety: John Kendrick

PATTERSON, Samuel   Sicily Poindexter
    M.B. January 11, 1773   Surety: Phil Poindexter
    Note: Sicily, daughter of Phillip Poindexter, Sr.

PATILLO, Samuel H.   Sally E. Phillips
    M.B. December 15, 1808   Surety: John C. Phillips
    Minister: James Meacham
    Consent: Pettus Phillips, relation not stated

PATILLO, Williamson   Jane Phillips
    M.B. July 13, 1808   Surety: Martin Phillips
    Minister: James Meacham

PAULL, James   Elizabeth Brook, Spinster
    M.B. February 12, 1776   Surety: Dudley Brook

PEARSON, Littleberry   Nanny Thomas
    M.B. December 1, 1786   Surety: Peter Thomas

PEARSON, Thomas, Jr.   Mary Delony
    M.B. September 19, 1768   Surety: Henry Delony
    Note: Mary, daughter of Henry Delony

PEEBLES, Thomas E.   Susanna P. Lucas
    M.B. March 20, 1804   Surety: William Parham

PEETE, Edwin H.   Nancy Speed
    M.B. January 8, 1807   M. January 13, 1807
    Minister: James Meacham   Surety: Charles Ogburn
    Consent: James Wilson guardian of Nancy

PENNINGTON, Drury   Polly Quarles
    M.B. December 6, 1809   Surety: John Wright

PENNINGTON, Philip   Patty Floyd
    M.B. January 29, 1787   Surety: John Saunders

PENNINGTON, Philip   Mary Burton
    M.B. May 31, 1798   M. June 14, 1798
    Minister: Ebenezer Macgowan   Surety: John Hubbard

PENNINGTON, Robert   Frances Finch
    M.B. January 26, 1787   Surety: Sherwood Smith

PENNINGTON, Walter   Polly Mabry
    M.B. December 22, 1802   Surety: Isham Nance, Jr.

PENTICOST, Scarborough   Phebe Lockett
    M.B. February 8, 1790   M. February 18, 1790
    Minister: John Williams   Surety: Daniel D. Watkins

PERKINSON, Rowlett   Susanna Pettus
    M.B. January 19, 1798   Surety: Matthew Pettus
    Minister: William Creath

PERKINSON, William   Mary Pettus
    M.B. February 8, 1790   Surety: Thomas Pettus

PETTIPOOL, Wiltshire Gromarin   Martha Ingram
    M.B. December 21, 1792   Surety: William Green
    Consent: Pines Ingram, father of Martha

PETTUS, Horatio   Mary S. Poindexter
    M.B. December 9, 1799   M. December 17, 1799
    Minister: Edward Almand   Surety: William Pettus
    Note: Mary Stephens, daughter of Phillip and Sarah
          Crymes Poindexter

PETTUS, John   Elizabeth Walker Pettus
    M.B. August 12, 1782   Surety: Thomas Pettus, Jr.
    Note: Elizabeth, daughter of Thomas Pettus

PETTUS, William   Betsy Ann Poindexter
    M.B. March 9, 1789   Surety: Samuel Hopkins, Jr.
    Note: Betsy Ann, daughter of Phillip and Sarah
          (Crymes) Poindexter

PETTWAY, John   Martha Alexander
    M.B. August 11, 1792   Surety: John Alexander
    Note: John Pettway of Warren County, N. C.

PHILLIPS, Archibald   Mary Hanserd
    M.B. November 26, 1795   Surety: Richard Hanserd

PHILLIPS, Dabney, Jr.   Martha Hutcheson
    M.B. January 6, 1801   Surety: William Brown
    Consent: Dabney Phillips, Sr., father of Dabney
    Consent: Charles Hutcheson, father of Martha
    Minister: William Creath

PHILLIPS, Dyer   Patience Clay
    M.B. December 18, 1786   Surety: Thomas Dawson
    Consent: Charles Clay, father of Patience

PHILLIPS, John   Fanny Walker
    M.B. September 10, 1798   M. September 16, 1798
    Minister: Alexander Hay.   Surety: Theophilus Feild
    Note: John Phillips of Prince George County
    Note: Theophilus Feild of Brunswick County

PHILLIPS, Jonathon   Martha Abernathy
    M.B. December 20, 1809   Surety: Liles Abernathy

PHILLIPS, Martin   Lucy Suggett
    M.B. November 5, 1808   Surety: John Hutcheson

PHILLIPS, Pettus   Rebeccah Coleman
    M.B. March 6, 1788   Surety: Lewis Parham
    Minister: Thomas Scott
    Note: Rebeccah, daughter of Cluverius Coleman

PHILLIPS, William   Rachel Edmundson
    M.B. October 14, 1793   Surety: George B. Hamner
    Consent: Samuel Edmundson, father of Rachel

PHILLIPS, William   Betsy Turner
    M.B. December 20, 1799   Surety: Matthew Turner, Jr.
    Minister: William Creath
    Consent: John Turner, father of Betsy

PINSON, Joseph   Mary Jones
    M.B. May 12, 1794   Surety: Arthur Atkinson
    Minister: James Read
    Consent: Richard Jones, father of Mary

PINSON, Thomas   Lucy Johnston
    M.B. February 12, 1810   Surety: Caleb Johnston

POARCH, Independence   Lucy Hudson
    M.B. August 8, 1801   M. August 13, 1801
    Minister: James Meacham   Surety: Thomas Webb

POARCH, Independence   Patsy Ellis
    M.B. February 2, 1807   Surety: Morris Green Burton

POARCH, Isham   Nancy Matthews
    M.B. January 2, 1802   M. January 6, 1802
    Minister: James Meacham   Surety: Benjamin W. Hudson

POINDEXTER, George   Nancy Hinton
    M.B. December 24, 1791   December 27, 1791
    Minister: John Williams   Surety: Randolph Westbrook
    Note: George, son of Phillip and Sarah (Crymes)
          Poindexter

POINDEXTER, Philip   Jane Goode
    M.B. June 13, 1768   Surety: Richard Witton, Jr.
    Consent: Edward Goode, father of Jane
    Note: Phillip Poindexter, Jr.

POINDEXTER, Philip   Mary Hinton
    M.B. August 12, 1799   Surety: Thomas Dance
    Note: Phillip Poindexter, Jr., half-brother of George

POOL, Alexander   Angelina Crowder
    M.B. October 11, 1790   Surety: Thomas Norment

POOLE, Mitchell   Nancy Christopher
    M.B. August 16, 1797   Surety: Turner Sharp

POOLE, William, Jr.   Rebecca Tanner
    M.B. January 17, 1797   M. January 18, 1797
    Minister: John Loyd   Surety: Thomas Tanner

POTTER, Abraham   Sarah Hawkins, Spinster
    M.B. February 6, 1771   Surety: John Potter

POTTER, Donaldson   Jane Wright
    M.B. September 3, 1804   M. September 6, 1804
    Minister: James Meacham   Surety: Edmund Clements

POWELL, William   Lucinda Rainey
    M.B. February 21, 1810   Surety: William Cook

POYTHRESS, Lewis   Elizabeth Giles
    M.B. December 26, 1792   M. December 27, 1792
    Minister: John Loyd   Surety: Meredith Poythress

POYTHRESS, Lewis   Rebecca B. Taylor
    M.B. April 9, 1802   Surety: Thomas Watson
    Minister: James Meacham

POYTHRESS, Meredith   Edith Cleaton
    M.B. July 14, 1781   Surety: William Cleaton

POYTHRESS, William   Ann Bently
    M.B. November 10, 1802   Surety: Thomas Rogers

PRESTON, Joshua   Lisha Feagins
    M.B. December 18, 1792   M. December 20, 1792
    Minister: John Loyd   Surety: John Saunders
    Note:Joshua Preston of Brunswick County

PRICE, Pugh Williamson   Elizabeth Williamson
    M.B. July 4, 1794   M. July 5, 1794
    Minister: William Richards   Surety: Josiah Price
    Consent: Robert Williamson, father of Elizabeth
    Note: Pugh W. Price of Prince Edward County

PRITCHETT, John   Susanna Cox
    M.B. December 14, 1795   M. December 23, 1795
    Minister: William Creath   Surety: William Hudson

PRITCHETT, Thomas, Jr.   Sally Hunt Hatsell
    M.B. August 7, 1798   M. August 10, 1798
    Minister: Matthew L. Easter   Surety: Edward Hatsell

PUCKETT, Banister   Betsy Page
    M.B. January 7, 1801   Surety: Isaac Bowen

PUCKETT, John   Jane Hopkins
    M.B. February 28, 1792   Surety: John Farrar

PULLIAM, Benjamin   Ann Hester
    M.B. March 8, 1784   Surety: Stephen Mabry

PULLIAM, Byrd   Susanna Phillips
    M.B. April 8, 1791   Surety: James Pulliam
    Minister: James Read

PULLIAM, John   Elizabeth Wilson
    M.B. September 11, 1775   Surety: Benjamin Pulliam

PULLIAM, Richard   Martha Mealer
    M.B. October 1, 1791   M. October 6, 1791
    Minister: James Read   Surety: Elijah Graves

PULLY, James   Lucy Moss
    M.B. December 21, 1805   Surety: David Moss

PULLY, William   Margaret Lawrence
    M.B. November 26, 1784   Surety: Hubbard Ferrell

PURYEAR, Elijah   Elizabeth Overton
    M.B. December 2, 1802   M. December 9, 1802
    Minister: Edward Almand   Surety: John Overton, Jr.

PURYEAR, Hezekiah   Kitty Hayes
    M.B. January 10, 1803   M. February 17, 1803
    Minister: Matthew Dance   Surety: Thomas Puryear

PURYEAR, James   Milly Moseley
    M.B. December 12, 1808   Surety: John Puryear

PURYEAR, John, Jr.   *
    M.B. June 20, 178-_   Johannah _____
    Surety: Samuel Puryear
    * Bond mutilated and only names on left legible

PURYEAR, John, Jr.   Sally S. Clausel
    M.B. October 24, 1799   Surety: Hezekiah Puryear
    Minister: William Creath

PURYEAR, John   Polly Hudson
    M.B. December 12, 1808   Surety: Samuel Hudson
    Minister: William Richards

PURYEAR, Peter   Phebe Burton
    M.B. December 10, 1792   Surety: Thomas Crowder

PURYEAR, Reuben   Martha Clausel
    M.B. December 23, 1791   M. December 27, 1791
    Minister: William Creath   Surety: James T. Hayes

PURYEAR, Samuel   Frances Clausel
    M.B. January 17, 1786   Richard Richard Clausel

PURYEAR, Samuel   Sally Stith Puryear
    M.B. September 20, 1810   Surety: Mackintosh Puryear
    Consent: Sarah Puryear, mother of Sally

PURYEAR, Semour   Sarah Royster
    M.B. April 10, 1775   Surety: John Puryear

PURYEAR, Seymour   Fanny Vaughan
    M.B. March 11, 1807   Surety: Wiley Burrus
    Consent: Nancy Foster, aunt of Fanny Vaughan

PURYEAR, Thomas   Patsy Harris
    M.B. March 25, 1801   M. April 2, 1801
    Minister: William Richards   Surety: Allen Harris
    Consent: Reuben Harris, father of Patsy

PURYEAR, Thomas   Elizabeth Marshall
    M.B. May 13, 1805   M. May 23, 1805
    Minister: William Richards   Surety: Francis Lockett

PURYEAR, William   Rebecca Carleton
    M.B. September 22, 1785   Surety: John Farrar
    Consent: Thomas Carleton, father of Rebecca

QUARLES, Williamson   Polly Benford
    M.B. January 14, 1806   Surety: Thomas Benford

RAGLAND, Abner   Nancy Fox
    M.B. March 3, 1799   M. March 5, 1799
    Minister: Ebenezer Macgowan   Surety: Richard Fox

RAGSDALE, Anthony   Anne Wells
    M.B. October 1, 1793   M. October 3, 1793
    Minister: William Creath   Surety: William Westbrook
    Consent: David Wells, father of Anne

RAGSDALE, Cornelius   Frances Mealer
    M.B. October 5, 1795   M. October 15, 1795
    Minister: William Richards   Surety: William Hundley

RAGSDALE, Drury   Susanna Mealer
    M.B. December 22, 1785   Surety: Thomas Wilbourn

RAGSDALE, Richard   Susanna Allen
    M.B. November 12, 1792   M. December 1, 1792
    Minister: Edward Almand   Surety: Robert Harris

RAGSDALE, Richard   Judith Hudson
    M.B. May 23, 1799   Surety: Richeson Farrar

RAGSDALE, Richard   Barsheba Bishop
    M.B. February 8, 1802   Surety: Littleberry Carter
    Minister: William Creath

RAINEY, Buckner   Rebecca Holmes
    M.B. June 12, 1780   Surety: Samuel Lark

RAINEY, Edmond   Polly H. Morgan
    M.B. October 21, 1807   Surety: Starling Morgan

RAINEY, Francis   Judith Lambert
    M.B. January 7, 1797   Surety: Mark Lambert Jackson

RAINEY, Frederick   Molly Morgan
    M.B. May 10, 1775   Surety: John Tabb

RAINEY, Isham   Betsy Morgan
    M.B. January 20, 1789   M. January 21, 1789
    Minister: Phillip Cox   Surety: Frederick Rainey

RAINEY, Robert   Levisy Crowder
    M.B. March 27, 1805   Surety: Nathaniel Crowder

RAINEY, Smith   Ann Standley
    M.B. December 31, 1796   M. January 4, 1797
    Minister: John Loyd   Surety: James Standley

RAINEY, Williamson   Edith Morgan
    M.B. November 23, 1779   Surety: Francis Rainey
    Consent: Reuben Morgan, relation not stated

RAINEY, Williamson   Martha Cook
    M.B. December 22, 1810   Surety: Charles D. Cleaton
    Consent: John Cook, Sr., father of Martha

RANSOM, James   Mary Hayes
    M.B. July 9, 1787   Surety: James T. Hayes
    Note: James Ransom of Amelia County

RAVENSCROFT, John Stark   Anne Spottswood Burwell
    M.B. August 13, 1792   Surety: William Hepburn
    Note: Anne, daughter of Lewis Burwell

READER, Jephthah   Winny Harrison
    M.B. January 10, 1803   M. January 19, 1803
    Minister: William Richards   Sur: Greenwood Harrison

READER, Jehu   Phebe Robards
    M.B. July 13, 1801   M. July 21, 1801
    Minister: William Richards   Surety: James Wilson

READER, Robert   Mary Mullins
    M.B. December 25, 1792   M. December 27, 1792
    Minister: John Williams   Surety: James Hudson

READER, Thomas   Lucy Mullins
    M.B. December 10, 1798   M. December 13, 1798
    Minister: William Richards   Surety: Richard Hughes

REAMS, Jeremiah   Dolly Fowler
    M.B. December 15, 1800   Surety: Starling Fowler

REAGAN, John F.   Catharine Evans
    M.B. October 5, 1791   M. October 23, 1791
    Minister: Edward Almand   Surety: William Taylor

REAMY, Abraham   Susanna Hudson
    M.B. March 13, 1809   M. March 16, 1809
    Minister: William Richards   Surety: William Harris

REAMY, Thomas A.   Phebe Burton
    M.B. January 13, 1800   M. January 16, 1800
    Minister: William Richards   Surety: James Wilson

REDDING, Ezekiel   Rebecca Mason
     M.B. April 18, 1791   Surety: Thomas Marriott

REEKES, Benjamin   Lucy Ingram
     M.B. August 12, 1801   Surety: Richard Crowder
     Minister: William Creath

REEKES, James   Sally Holmes
     M.B. December 13, 1796   M. December 15, 1796
     Minister: John Neblett   Surety: John Walton
     Note: Sally (Sarah), daughter of Samuel Holmes

RICHARDS, William   Mary Evans
     M.B. December 14, 1801   Surety: Richard Jeffries
     Minister: William Creath

RIDOUT, Gordon   Sally Grigg
     M.B. February 6, 1802   M. February 10, 1802
     Minister: James Meacham   Surety: William Ezell
     Consent: Lewis Grigg, father of Sally

RIGGINS, John   Mary Hutt
     M.B. May 14, 1798   M. May 17, 1798
     Minister: Edward Almand   Surety: William Hilton

RIVES, William   Mary Turner
     M.B. January 1, 1788   Surety: Nicholas Bilbo
     Consent: Thomas Rives, father of William
     Consent: Stephen Turner, father of Mary

ROBERTS, Absolom   Susannah B. Collier
     M.B. September 3, 1807   Surety: Phillip Roberts

ROBERTS, Anselm   Nancy Bottom
     M.B. July 22, 1806   M. July 23, 1806
     Minister: James Meacham   Surety: Hughberry Nanney

ROBERTS, Dennis   Lucy Roberts
     M.B. December 21, 1798   M. December 25, 1798
     Minister: William Creath   Surety: William Roberts

ROBERTS, George   Polly Stembridge
     M.B. October 15, 1810   Surety: James Stembridge

ROBERTS, John   * Leanner Allen
     M.B. May 21, 1799   Surety: William Allen
     * Leanna Allen

ROBERTS, Lewis   * Siller May
     M.B. October 17, 1797   Surety: Henry Roberts
     * Priscilla May

ROBERTS, Phillip   Tabitha Watson
    M.B. December 29, 1802   Surety: Thomas Shelton

ROBERTS, Robert   Elizabeth Rook
    M.B. February 20, 1799   Surety: Starling Morgan

ROBERTS, William, Jr.   Frances Roberts
    M.B. August 21, 1802   Surety: Phillip Roberts
    Minister: William Creath

ROBERTSON, Allen   Amasa Burrus
    M.B. September 4, 1801   Surety: Henry Royall
    Minister: William Creath

ROBERTSON, Drury   Mary Winfield
    M.B. February 4, 1786   Surety: Matthew Turner

ROBERTSON, John Moody   Mary E. Lamb
    M.B. March 1, 1792   Surety: Pines Ingram
    Consent: Joseph Boswell (grandfather), guardian of
        Mary E. Lamb

ROBERTSON, Leoderick   Nancy Thomas
    M.B. March 11, 1806   Surety: John Allgood
    Minister: Thomas Hardie

ROBERTSON, Nathaniel   Nancy Crews
    M.B. December 9, 1799   Surety: Richard H. Walker

ROBERTSON, Thomas   Elizabeth Roberts
    M.B. June 16, 1787   Surety: Thomas Roberts

ROBINSON, Clack   Elanor Young
    M.B. October 11, 1809   Surety: Walter Langley
    Minister: James Meacham

ROBINSON, James   Martha Winfield
    M.B. November 2, 1803   M. November 9, 1803
    Minister: James Meacham   Surety: William Thomas
    Consent: Joshua Winfield, father of Martha

ROFFE, Edward   Miney Burton
    M.B. July 16, 1787   Surety: William Johnson
    Consent: Robert Burton, father of Miney

ROFFE, Ingram   Agnes Love
    M.B. February 17, 1803   Surety: William Love
    Consent: Charles Love, father of Agnes

ROFFE, John   Martha Simmons
    M.B. January 1, 1794   M. January 2, 1794
    Minister: William Creath   Surety: Samuel Simmons

ROFFE, Melchizedeck   Ann Dodson
    M.B. December 12, 1800   Surety: William Dodson

ROFFE, William   Sarah Knight
    M.B. October 9, 1794   M. October 19, 1794
    Minister: William Creath   Surety: Ingram Vaughan

ROBERTS, Stephen   Martha Gregory
    M.B. August 20, 1810   M. August 30, 1810
    Minister: David McCargo   Surety: Nathaniel Fowlkes

ROSE, Anderson   Polly Puryear
    M.B. July 9, 1804   Surety: Valentine McCutcheon

ROSS, Robert   Lucy Arnold
    M.B. November 14, 1792   M. November 22, 1792
    Minister: John Neblett   Surety: Elisha Arnold

ROTTENBERRY, Charles   Sally Glover
    M.B. December 4, 1798   M. December 24, 1798
    Minister: Ebenezer Macgowan   Surety: James Burton

ROTTENBERRY, McDaniel   Nancy Bowen
    M.B. March 3, 1797   M. March 8, 1797
    Minister: John Loyd   Surety: John Thomerson

ROTTENBERRY, Winn   Elizabeth F. Hudgins
    M.B. November 26, 1801   Surety: Abel Edmunds
    Consent: James Hudgins, father of Elizabeth

ROWLAND, Richard   Rachel Ragsdale
    M.B. December 10, 1781   Surety: Henry Robertson

ROWLETT, Thompson   Polly Dodson
    M.B. November 9, 1805   M. November 18, 1805
    Minister: James Meacham

ROYAL, Henry   Letty Hutt
    M.B. July 18, 1805   Surety: Peter Puryear

ROYAL, Joseph   Elizabeth Thomas
    M.B. August 11, 1794   M. September 14, 1794
    Minister: William Creath   Surety: Matthew Clements

ROYAL, William   Sally Robertson
    M.B. June 10, 1799   Surety: Allen Robertson

ROYSTER, Charles   Elizabeth Burrows
    M.B. November 14, 1803   Surety: Jordan Mason
    Consent: William T. Burrows, father of Elizabeth

ROYSTER, Clark   Lucy Apperson
    M.B. October 11, 1802   M. October 12, 1802
    Minister: Baalam Ezell   Surety: Archibald Clarke

ROYSTER, Dennis   Rebecca Royster
    M.B. January 17, 1807   Surety: Stark Daniel
    Minister: William Richards

ROYSTER, Francis   Ann Roberts
    M.B. December 13, 1802   Surety: Valentine McCutcheon
    Minister: William Creath

ROYSTER, George   Susanna Hall
    M.B. August 7, 1790   Surety: William Marshall

ROYSTER, Henry   Frances Draper
    M.B. November 8, 1790   Surety: Joseph Royster

ROYSTER, Joseph   Elizabeth Draper
    M.B. December 12, 1791   M. December 27, 1791
    Minister: James Read   Surety: Holeman Rice

ROYSTER, Wilkins   Mary Robertson
    M.B. February 13, 1797   M. February 18, 1797
    Minister: William Richards   Sur: Samuel Hester, Jr.

RUDD, John   Elizabeth Edmundson
    M.B. October 15, 1810   M. October 25, 1810
    Minister: William Richards   Surety: Brown Avory

RUDDER, Alexander   Elizabeth McLaughlin
    M.B. December 21, 1791   M. December 22, 1791
    Minister: James Read   Surety: Edward Brodnax
    Note: Edward Brodnax of Lunenburg County

RUFFIN, Theoderick Bland   Susanna Murray
    M.B. January 14, 1788   Surety: Jesse Brown
    Consent: William Yates, guardian of Susanna
    Minister: Thomas Scott

RUSSELL, Burwell   Prudence Hogan
    M.B. January 11, 1785   Surety: William McQuie

RUSSELL, Jeremiah   Jilley Atkins
    M.B. August 26, 1795   M. August 27, 1795
    Minister: John Loyd   Surety: James Atkins
    Note: Jeremiah Russell of Brunswick County

RUSSELL, Jeremiah   Sarah Thompson
    M.B. December 21, 1809   Surety: Theophilus Russell

RUSSELL, Jesse   Rebekah Harris
  M.B. December 11, 1798   M. December 20, 1798
  Minister: Charles Ogburn   Surety: Stephen Evans

RUSSELL, John   Catherine Stone
  M.B. March 30, 1801   M. April 2, 1801
  Minister: John Neblett   Surety: Benjamin Mitchell

RUSSELL, Mark   Mary Puckett
  M.B. December 3, 1785   Surety: John Daly

RYLAND, Hundley   Nancy Walker
  M.B. January 11, 1802   Surety: John Brown

RYLAND, Iverson   Lucy Dortch
  M.B. February 23, 1784   Surety: Nathaniel Moss

RYLAND, John   *
  M.B. January 11, 1786   Surety: Thomas Adams
  * Noy named in bond

RYLAND, Thomas   Martha Coleman
  M.B. December 16, 1803   Surety: John Ryland

SADLER, William   Avarilla Greenwood
  M.B. November 12, 1798   Surety: John Greenwood
  Consent: Thomas Greenwood, father of Avarilla

SALLEY, James (Salle')   Audrey Keeton
  M.B. December 9, 1793   M. December 19, 1793
  Minister: William Creath   Surety: Reuben Cardin

SAMUEL, Andrew   Delina Tanner
  M.B. May 11, 1786   Surety: Thomas Tanner

SANDIFER, Henry   Martha Taylor
  M.B. December 14, 1785   Surety: Samuel Durham

SAUNDERS, Benjamin   Mary Anne Moore
  M.B. February 19, 1791   Surety: Philip B. Moore

SAUNDERS, George   Hally Emery
  M.B. December 3, 1804   Surety: Thomas Saunders

SAUNDERS, Thomas   Polly Morris
  M.B. December 19, 1803   Surety: Edward Morris
  Minister: William Creath
  Consent: John Saunders, father of Thomas
  Consent: Jesse Morris, Sr., father of Polly

SAVAGE, John   Mary Taylor
    M.B. May 1, 1787   Surety: James Day

SCOTT, Avory   Elizabeth Chavous
    M.B. January 9, 1809   M. January 21, 1809
    Minister: William Richards   Surety: Frederick Ivey
    Consent: Elizabeth Chavous, mother of Elizabeth

SCOTT, Robert   Elizabeth Pettus
    M.B. September 8, 1806   Surety: William Pettus
    Consent: Samuel Pettus, Senr., relation not stated
    Note: Elizabeth, daughter of Samuel Pettus

SCOTT, Samuel   Martha Henly
    M.B. January 5, 1792   M. January 11, 1792
    Minister: William Creath   Surety: William Johnson
    Note: Samuel Scott of Dinwiddie County

SELDEN, Joseph   Mary Burwell
    M.B. April 11, 1785   Surety: Samuel Goode

SEWARD, Isaac   Lucy Valentine
    M.B. October 25, 1803   Surety: Isham Valentine

SEWARD, John   Betsy Malone
    M.B. June 2, 1771   Surety: Drury Malone

SEWARD, John, Jr.   Sarah Hanserd
    M.B. December 6, 1799   M. December 11, 1799
    Minister: James Meacham   Surety: Richard Hanserd

SHACKLEFORD, Zachariah   Susannah Allgood Salle'
    M.B. October 9, 1797   Surety: John Allgood
    Minister: William Creath

SHARP, Turner   Martha Jones
    M.B. January 24, 1797   M. January 26, 1797
    Minister: William Creath   Surety: James Elam
    Consent: Richard Jones, father of Martha

SHARP, Turner   Elizabeth Jones
    M.B. May 11, 1807   M. May 14, 1807
    Minister: William Richards   Surety: Martin Gillespie
    Consent: Charles Jones, guardian of Elizabeth
    Note: Elizabeth, daughter of Richard Jones, deceased

SHAW, John   Susanna Carter
    M.B. August 4, 1790   Surety Drury Creedle

SHAW, John   Patsy Crowder
    M.B. November 10, 1800   Surety: Thomas Marriott
    Minister: William Creath

SHEARER, James   Nancy Allen
    M.B. November 13, 1797   M. November 30, 1797
    Minister: William Richards   Surety: John Cox

SHELL, Freeman   Becky Tisdale
    M.B. March 18, 1806   M. March 21, 1806
    Minister: Charles Ogburn   Surety: Bartlett Cox

SHELL, Herman   Martha Eppes
    M.B. October 9, 1790   M. October 19, 1790
    Minister: William Heath   Surety: John Eppes
    Note: Herman Shell of Brunswick County

SHELL, John   Lizzy Malone
    M.B. May 28, 1786   Surety: Hardy Jones

SHELTON, Edward   Phebe Walker
    M.B. December 22, 1803   Surety: Bartley Cheatham

SHELTON, James   Nancy Marshall
    M.B. February 12, 1810   M. February 14, 1810
    Minister: William Richards   Surety: Phillip Lockett

SHELTON, Thomas   Martha Watson
    M.B. December 29, 1799   M. December 31, 1799
    Minister: Ebenezer Macgowan   Surety: Jordan Bennett

SHORT, Batte   Patsy Lett
    M.B. May 30, 1791   Surety: James Bing

SHORT, Batte   Seller Murdock
    M.B. November 2, 1798   M. November 9, 1798
    Minister: Charles Ogburn   Surety: John Carroll

SHORT, Edmund   Susanna Bilbo
    M.B. August 6, 1787   Surety: John Bilbo

SHORT, Freeman   Elizabeth Evans
    M.B. September 1, 1808   Surety: George Finch

SHORT, Isaac   Susanna Toone
    M.B. January 12, 1795   Surety: John Stegall

SHORT, Jacob   Phebe Finch
    M.B. October 23, 1794   Surety: William Finch
    Minister: John Loyd

SHORT, John   Rebecca Goode
    M.B. January 28, 1807   Surety: Edward Holloway
    Minister: James Meacham

SHORT, Wyatt   Mary Adams
    M.B. December 11, 1809   M. December 28, 1809
    Minister: James Meacham   Surety: Richard M. Allen

SIMMONS, James   Mourning Lark
    M.B. January 3, 1805   Surety: James Noel

SIMMONS, John   Elizabeth Baugh
    M.B. September 23, 1790   M. September 30, 1790
    Minister: John Easter   Surety: James Baugh
    Note: Elizabeth, daughter of James and Agnes Baugh

SIMMONS, Joseph   Elizabeth Harrison
    M.B. May 8, 1797   M. May 11, 1797
    Minister: Charles Ogburn   Surety: Samuel Simmons
    Consent: John and Sarah Ogburn, guardians of
            Elizabeth Harrison

SIMMONS, Samuel   Elizabeth Coleman
    M.B. August 7, 1795   M. August 15, 1795
    Minister: Charles Ogburn   Surety: Thomas Coleman

SIMS, Leonard   Sarah Swepson
    M.B. March 12, 1770   Surety: Richard Swepson

SIMS, Saunders   Lucy Hutcheson
    M.B. January 21, 1794   M. January 28, 1794
    Minister: William Creath   Surety: Charles Hutcheson

SIMPSON, Edwin   Mahala Stewart
    M.B. December 12, 1808   Surety: Saunders Harris

SINGLETON, John   Ann Daly
    M.B. September 4, 1793   M. September 5, 1793
    Minister: John Loyd   Surety: Daniel Daly

SINGLETON, John   Rebeccah Crook
    M.B. October 8, 1801   Surety: James Nash

SINGLETON, John   Frances Johnson
    M.B. December 19, 1810   M. December 20, 1810
    Minister: Name not given   Surety: John Curtis

SINGLETON, Robert   Polly Thomason
    M.B. December 30, 1795   M. December 31, 1795
    Minister: John Loyd   Surety: William Barrett
    Note: Polly, daughter of John and Mary Thomason

SINGLETON, William   Susanna Gwaltney
    M.B. January 13, 1798   Surety: Richard Stone
    Consent: William Gwaltney, father of Susanna

SLATE, Robert   Elizabeth Vaughan
    M.B. November 12, 1802   Surety: John Saunders
    Minister: William Creath
    Note: Robert Slate of Brunswick County

SMALL, George   Edith Overby
    M.B. March 30, 1799   Surety: Charles Hudson

SMITH, Anderson   Elizabeth Maryann Avary
    M.B. June 9, 1783   Surety: John Avary
    Note: Elizabeth, daughter of John Avary

SMITH, Archer   Mary Brame
    M.B. April 11, 1796   Surety: James Norment
    Minister: William Richards   M. April 21, 1796
    Note: Archer, son of John and Martha Smith

SMITH, Augustine, Jr.   Nancy Rudd
    M.B. February 8, 1790   Surety: William Insco

SMITH, Benjamin   Caty Page
    M.B. April 2, 1803   Surety: Thomas Smith

SMITH, Daniel   Patsy Poindexter
    M.B. December 10, 1792   Surety: Robert Smith
    Minister: Edward Almand
    Note: Daniel, son of John and Martha Smith
    Note: Patsy, daughter of Phillip Poindexter, Sr.

SMITH, Ichabod   Lucy Pennington
    M.B. October 31, 1795   M. November 15, 1795
    Minister: William Creath   Surety: Henry Pennington
    Note: Ichabod, son of John and Paulina Smith

SMITH, James   Elinor Hyde
    M.B. December 12, 1791   Surety: Robert Hyde
    Note: James, son of Jøhn and Martha Smith

SMITH, John   Nancy Smith
    M.B. March 29, 1791   Surety: Augustine Smith

SMITH, John   Sally Ellis
    M.B. January 29, 1796   M. January 30, 1796
    Minister: John Loyd   Surety: John Loyd

SMITH, John Prior   Susanna Smith
    M.B. October 7, 1776   Surety: Achilles Jeffries
    Note: Susanna, daughter of Drury Smith

SMITH, John P.   Polly Oslin
    M.B. October 30, 1801   Surety: Isaac Oslin

SMITH, Joseph
    M.B. September 11, 1792
    Minister: Rice Haggard

                        Elizabeth Burnett
        M. September 20, 1792
    Surety: Silvanus Ingram

SMITH, Joshua
    M.B. January 6, 1801

                            Olive Brown
    Surety: William Hutcheson

SMITH, Matthew
    M.B. November 24, 1787

                        Sibbie Lambert
    Surety: Joseph Lambert

SMITH, Obadiah
    M.B. May 22, 1798
    Minister: Alexander Hay
    Consent: Tabitha Wilson, mother and guardian of
           Tabitha
    Note: Obadiah, son of Peartree Smith

                        Tabitha Wilson
        M. May 24, 1798
    Surety: James Wilson

SMITH, Robert
    M.B. January 8, 1787
    Note: Robert, son of John and Martha Smith

                        Nancy Norment
    Surety: Thomas Norment

SMITH, Samuel Hancock
    M.B. July 24, 1806
    Minister: William Richards

              Jane Wright Russell
        M. July 26, 1806
    Surety: Thomas A. Jones

SMITH, Sherwood
    M.B. December 21, 1786
    Note: Faith, daughter of Isaac Holmes, deceased

                        Faithy Holmes
    Surety: William Starling

SMITH, Thomas
    M.B. September 28, 1795
    Minister: Charles Ogburn

                        Mary Wilson
        M. October 1, 1795
    Surety: James Day

SMITH, Thomas
    M.B. March 15, 1806

                        Patsy Hubbard
    Surety: John Hubbard

SMITH, William
    M.B. October 13, 1787

                        Anne Pitts
    Surety: William Nowell

SMITH, William H.
    M.B. February 12, 1808
    Note: Mary, daughter of Aurelius and Nancy (Turner)
           Walker

                        Mary Walker
    Surety: Matthew Walker

SMITHSON, Bartley
    M.B. November 30, 1799
    Minister: Matthew Dance
    Consent: William Weatherford, father of Sarah

              Sarah Weatherford
        M. December 4, 1799
    Surety: Freeman Weatherford

SMITHSON, Briant
    M.B. June 13, 1796
    Minister: William Creath

                        Dolly Burton
        M. June 16, 1796
    Surety: Peter Puryear

SMITHSON, Charles   Betsy Cheatham
    M.B. December 8, 1800   Surety: Samuel Cheatham

SOMMERVILL, George   Elenor H. Birtchett
    M.B. March 23, 1811   Surety: Henry Hicks
    Minister: George Micklejohn

SPAIN, Abraham   Elizabeth Allen
    M.B. May 6, 1795   M. May 7, 1795
    Minister: William Richards   Surety: Henderson Wade

SPAIN, Daniel   Judith Allen
    M.B. November 18, 1802   M. November 19, 1802
    Minister: William Richards   Surety: Abraham Spain

SPAIN, Thomas   Elizabeth Haskins
    M.B. January 6, 1797   M. January 7, 1797
    Minister: Edward Almand   Surety: William Lucas

SPAIN, Thomas   Nancy Stewart
    M.B. September 14, 1801   Surety: Frederick Ivey

SPAIN, William   Judith Harris
    M.B. December 13, 1802   M. December 27, 1802
    Minister: William Richards   Surety: James Clack

SPARKS, William   Judith Thompson
    M.B. January 9, 1804   M. January 19, 1804
    Minister: William Richards   Surety: Bernard Thompson

SPEAKS, George   Martha Matthews
    M.B. November 8, 1809   Surety: John Matthews

SPEED, John James   Lucy Swepson
    M.B. January 26, 1801   M. January 29, 1801
    Minister: William Richards   Surety: G. H. Baskervill

SPEED, John   Polly Wade
    M.B. July 3, 1798   Surety: Joseph Speed, Jr.
    Consent: Joseph Townes, guardian of Polly Wade

SPEED, Robert   Polly A. Coleman
    M.B. January 15, 1809   Surety: William Coleman
    Note: Polly (Mary Ann), daughter of James Coleman,
          deceased

SPENCE, Thomas   Nancy Stewart
    M.B. September 14, 1801   Surety: Francis Ivey
    Minister: William Creath

SPURLOCK, William   Tempy Nanney
    M.B. December 9, 1798   M. December 27, 1798
    Minister: William Creath   Surety: William Roberts

SPURLOCK, Zachariah   Elizabeth Mealer
     M.B. October 13, 1792   Surety: John Farrar
     Minister: John Loyd

STAINBACK, Robert   Polly Andrews
     M.B. December 13, 1804   Surety: Isaac Arnold
     Note: Robert Stainback of Brunswick County

STANFIELD, Drew   Honora Heathcock
     M.B. December 13, 1803   Surety: George Guy

STEGALL, George   Mary F. Short
     M.B. January 23, 1799   Surety: Henry Finch
     Minister: John Neblett

STEGALL, John   Susanna Beddingfield
     M.B. December 12, 1786   Surety: William Finch

STEMBRIDGE, James   Elizabeth Gregory
     M.B. December 31, 1801   M. January 7, 1802
     Minister: William Richards   Surety: John Stembridge

STEMBRIDGE, John   Sally Graves
     M.B. December 24, 1803   M. December 28, 1803
     Minister: Edward Almand   Surety: Obadiah Belcher

STEWART, Archer   Jincy Chavous
     M.B. August 14, 1809   M. August 25, 1809
     Minister: James Meacham   Surety: Edward Brandon

STEWART, Bartlett   Elizabeth Drew
     M.B. October 21, 1807   Surety: George Guy

STEWART, Charles   Sarah Elam
     M.B. November 14, 1808   M. April 7, 1809
     Minister: William Richards   Surety: Frederick Ivey

STEWART, George   Jean Chandler
     M.B. December 27, 1797   Surety: Moses Stewart

STEWART, John Ginnet   Polly Manning
     M.B. December 9, 1794   Surety: Irby Chavous
     Consent: Susanna Chavous, mother of Polly

STEWART, Matthew   Priscilla Walden
     M.B. February 25, 1799   M. February 26, 1799
     Minister: Ebenezer Macgowan   Surety: William Chandler

STEWART, Matthew   Eliza Stewart
     M.B. February 8, 1802   Surety: Miles Dunston

STEWART, Thomas   Sarah Cattiler
     M.B. July 15, 1800   Surety: Richeson Farrar

116

STALCUP, Tobias   Lucy Pearce
    M.B. January 9, 1809   Surety: Baalam Ezell

STEWART, James, Jr.   Ryte Chavous
    M.B. February 11, 1788   Surety: James Stewart, Sr.

STONE, Asher   Frances Cox
    M.B. November 13, 1797   M. November 30, 1797
    Minister: William Richards   Surety: John Cox
    Note: Asher, son of William (Sr.) and Tabitha Stone

STONE, Drury   Nancy Hundley
    M.B. November 12, 1798   Surety: William Hundley

STONE, Elijah   Rebecca Roberts
    M.B. August 13, 1792   M. August 15, 1792
    Minister: William Creath   Surety: Thomas Roberts

STONE, James   Johanna Jones
    M.B. January 10, 1791   Surety: Daniel Jones
    Minister: James Read
    Note: Johanna, daughter of Captain Thomas Jones
    Note: Johanna, sister of Daniel Jones, surety

STONE, James   Elizabeth Griffin
    M.B. March 12, 1810   Surety: Elijah Griffin

STONE, John   Elizabeth Hutcheson
    M.B. December 11, 1797   Surety: William Stone

STONE, Jordan   Margaret Griffin
    M.B. December 17, 1803   Surety: Elijah Griffin

STONE, William, Jr.   Susanna Hutcheson
    M.B. November 21, 1795   M. November 26, 1795
    Minister: Charles Ogburn   Surety: Jesse Carsley
    Consent: William Stone, Sr., guardian of Susanna

STROUD, Willis   Elizabeth Blanton
    M.B. September 11, 1792   Surety: George Small
    Minister: John Loyd

STUART, James   Prescilla Stuart
    M.B. November 14, 1791   Surety: John Walden

STUART, Moses   Polly Walden
    M.B. December 20, 1788   Surety: Eaton Walden
    Consent: John Charles Walden, father of Polly

STUART, William   Keziah Corn
    M.B. _____ 21, ____ *   Surety: Robert Corn
    Note: William Stuart of Brunswick County
    * Marriage Bond mutilated and date illegible

STURDIVANT, Randal   Dicy Rainey
    M.B. May 27, 1776   Surety: Francis Rainey

STURDIVANT, Randolph   Mourning Lambert
    M.B. January 5, 1797   Surety: David Thomas
    Minister: John Loyd
    Consent: Joseph Lambert, father of Mourning

SWEPSON, Richard   (Mrs.) Mary Tabb
    M.B. April 12, 1779   Surety: Achilles Jeffries
    Note: Mary Tabb, widow of John Tabb (first Clerk of
        Mecklenburg County)

SWEPSON, William M.   Elizabeth I. Speed
    M.B. March 27, 1805   Surety: John James Speed

TABB, Edward L.   Elizabeth Blair Burwell
    M.B. January 31, 1791   Surety: G. H. Baskervill
    Consent: Lewis Burwell, father of Elizabeth
    Note: Edward, son of John and Mary Tabb

TALLEY, George   Lucy McDaniel
    M.B. December 12, 1787   Surety: James Moore
    Consent: John and Mary McDaniel, parents of Lucy

TALLEY, Grief   Lucy Curtis
    M.B. September 16, 1799   Surety: Drury Creedle
    Minister: Charles Ogburn

TALLEY, Larkin   Polly Blacketter
    M.B. September 27, 1805   Surety: Samuel Bugg

TALLEY, Russell   Elizabeth Creedle
    M.B. July 14, 1791   Surety: Bryant Creedle

TANNER, David   Martha Ferrell
    M.B. May 6, 1802   Surety: Hutchins Ferrell

TANNER, Jonathon   Mary Young
    M.B. June 5, 1798   Surety: Allen Young

TANNER, Ludwell   Lucy Holmes
    M.B. December 2, 1781   Surety: John Baskervill
    Note: Lucy, daughter of Isaac Holmes

TANNER, Richard   Nancy Andrews
    M.B. October 15, 1808   Surety: Varney Andrews
    Note: Nancy, daughter of Varney Andrews, Senr.

TARRY, George   Sarah Taylor
    M.B. December 7, 1790   Surety: Anderson Taylor

TARRY, Robert   Nancy Smith
     M.B. June 10, 1793   Surety: Joseph Townes
     Note: Nancy, daughter of Peartree Smith
     Note: Robert Tarry of Halifax County

TARRY, Samuel   Amey Pettus
     M.B. July 8, 1799   Surety: William Coleman

TARRY, Samuel   Mary Brown
     M.B. March 14, 1808   Surety: George Craighead
     Minister: James Meacham   M. March 16, 1808

TAYLOR, Absolom   Martha C. Barnett
     M.B. December 29, 1809   Surety: John Hudgins

TAYLOR, Clark   Elizabeth Whitehead
     M.B. February 13, 1786   Surety: Richard Swepson

TAYLOR, David   Rebecca Dortch
     M.B. May 9, 1778   Surety: William Taylor
     Note: Rebecca, daughter of David Dortch

TAYLOR, Goodwyn   Nancy Drumwright
     M.B. January 10, 1794   M. January 21, 1794
     Minister: John Loyd   Surety: William Drumwright

TAYLOR, Goodwyn   Elizabeth Davis
     M.B. May 5, 1802   Surety: David Dortch

TAYLOR, Howell   Susanna Young
     M.B. December 30, 1778   Surety: Samuel Young

TAYLOR, James, Jr.   Priscilla Fox
     M.B. December 9, 1801   M. December 10, 1801
     Minister: James Meacham   Surety: Josiah Floyd

TAYLOR, Jesse   Phebe Moody
     M.B. June 27, 1789   Surety: Francis Moody
     Consent: Henry Moody, father of Phebe
     Minister: Thomas Scott

TAYLOR, John   * Happy Cook
     M.B. January 5, 1802   Surety: Abel Dortch
     * Kerrenhappuck Cook

TAYLOR, Jones   Joice Lark
     M.B. April 11, 1780   Surety: John Holmes

TAYLOR, Joseph   Elizabeth Willis Goode
     M.B. February 29, 1796   M. March 1, 1796
     Minister: William Creath   Surety: Francis Jones
     Consent: Swepson Jeffries, guardian of Elizabeth

TAYLOR, Richard B.   Mary C. Gregory
    M.B. December 4, 1798   Surety: Richard Gregory

TAYLOR, Thomas   Sally Benford
    M.B. September 28, 1792   M. October 14, 1792
    Minister: John Loyd   Surety: William Drumwright

TAYLOR, Thomas   Lucy Crutchfield
    M.B. January 24, 1797   M. January 31, 1797
    Minister: John Loyd   Surety: William Drumwright

TAYLOR, Thomas   Sally Lark
    M.B. December 26, 1797   Surety: Samuel Lark

TAYLOR, Thomas   Martha Cocke Hamblin
    M.B. October 18, 1800   Surety: Reuben Vaughan
    Consent: Agnes Hamblin, mother and guardian of Martha
    Minister: John Cameron

TAYLOR, Thomas   Martha Leach
    M.B. August 5, 1808   Surety: Francis Gregory

TAYLOR, William   Elizabeth Holloway
    M.B. April 26, 1785   Surety: Samuel Durham

TAYLOR, William   Molly Gober
    M.B. July 4, 1798   Surety: John Gober

TAYLOR, William Ladd   Mary Ambrose
    M.B. December 2, 1785   Surety: William Drumwright
    Minister: John King

TEMPLE, Samuel   Susanna Coppedge
    M.B. November 11, 1793   M. November 14, 1793
    Minister: John Loyd   Surety: Charles Coppedge

TERRY, Roaling (Rowland)   Mary Watkins
    M.B. October 12, 1807   Surety: Overton Wiles

THOMAS, Bennett   Patsy Jones
    M.B. March 24, 1810   Surety: William Jones

THOMAS, Billy   Lucy Stuart
    M.B. April 10, 1786   M. April 20, 1786
    Minister: John Williams   Surety: Francis Stuart

THOMAS, William   Frances H. Carless
    M.B. December 20, 1790   M. December 24, 1790
    Minister: John King   Surety: Peter Thomas, Jr.

THOMASON, Banister   Mary Singleton
    M.B. July 25, 1795   M. July 30, 1795
    Minister: John Loyd   Surety: William Thomason
    Note: Banister, son of John and Mary Thomason

THOMASON, James   Molly Thompson
    M.B. December 4, 1804   Surety: David Hicks
    Note: James, son of John and Mary Thomason

THOMASON, William, Jr.   Patsy Laffoon
    M.B. February 7, 1805   Surety: William Thomason, Sr.

THOMPSON, Bernard   Milly Yates
    M.B. December 10, 1804   Surety: John Walton

THOMPSON, Charles   Frances Daly
    M.B. December 9, 1782   Surety: Phil Ricks

THOMPSON, James   Susanna Nunnery
    M.B. August 27, 1806   M. August 30, 1806
    Minister: Charles Ogburn   Surety: Daniel Tucker, Sr.

THOMPSON, James Mims   Nancy Jackson
    M.B. January 3, 1789   Surety: John Allen
    Consent: John Thompson, relation not stated
    Consent: Fleming and Elizabeth Jackson, parents

THOMPSON, John   Sarah Thompson
    M.B. May 8, 1775   Surety: Asa Oliver

THOMPSON, John   Phebe Tisdale
    M.B. January 12, 1795   Surety: William Thompson
    Minister: William Creath

THOMPSON, John   Nancy Burnett
    M.B. April 13, 1801   Surety: Richard Burnett
    Minister: William Creath

THOMPSON, John   * Mary Sally
    M.B. October 12, 1807   Surety: Stephen P'Pool
    * Mary Salle'

THOMPSON, Richard   Frances Anne Watts
    M.B. June 14, 1802   M. July 29, 1802
    Minister: Matthew Dance   Surety: Henry Ashton
    Consent: Anna Watts, mother of Frances

THOMPSON, Stith   Elizabeth Parker
    Minister: Henry Lester   M. July 24, 1785

THOMPSON, William   Nancy Butler
    M.B. December 27, 1802   Surety: James Thompson

THOMPSON, William   Thrudy Stewart
    M.B. November 11, 1805   Surety: Neely Stewart

THOMPSON, William   Mary Hailestock
    M.B. February 19, 1808   Surety: Abel Stewart

THREADGILL, Thomas   Tabitha Ingram
    M.B. September 9, 1782   Surety: Reuben Vaughan

TILLOTSON, Edward   Milly Gold
    M.B. February 2, 1808   Surety: John Hailey
    Consent: William Tillotson, father of Edward
    Consent: Thomas Hailey, stepfather of Milly
    Note: Milly, daughter of Daniel Gold, deceased

TILLOTSON, John   * Delphia Yancey
    M.B. January 16, 1801   Surety: Richard Murray
    * Philadelphia Yancey

TISDALE, John   Nancy Clark
    M.B. March 13, 1787   Surety: Thomas Clark

TOONE, Argelon   Mary Freeman
    M.B. October 13, 1783   Surety: James Hix

TOONE, James   Milly Daniel
    M.B. April 9, 1770   Surety: William Taylor
    Consent: William Daniel, father of Milly

TOONE, Lewis   Rebeccah Moore
    M.B. August 15, 1787   Surety: Francis Lewis

TOONE, Lewis   Millicent Richards
    M.B. February 11, 1805   Surety: Abraham Keen
    Minister: James Shelburne   M. March 4, 1805
    Consent: W. W. Richards, father of Millicent

TOONE, Tavener   Ann Marshall
    M.B. May 20, 1809   Surety: George Bilbo

TOONE, Thomas   Winny Garner
    M.B. August 11, 1800   M. August 21, 1800
    Minister: Edward Almand   Surety: Richard Brown
    Consent: James Garner, father of Winifred

TOONE, William   Elizabeth Hamblin
    M.B. March 22, 1786   Isaac Pully

TOWNES, Henry   Polly Davis
    M.B. December 31, 1784   Surety: William Townes
    Consent: Barton Davis, father of Polly

TOWNES, Joseph   Isabella Wade
    M.B. June 28, 1784   Surety: Henry Townes
    Note: Henry Townes of Halifax County

TOWNSEND, Peter   Lucy Hundley
    M.B. July 11, 1808   Surety: Willis Hundley

TRAYLOR, Cary   Elizabeth Thompson
    M.B. November 7, 1786   Surety: John Johnson

TRICE, Thomas   Mary Green
    M.B. August 11, 1777   Surety: Edmund Taylor, Gent.
    Note: Mary Green, widow of Thomas Green

TUCKER, Daniel   Jincy Cardin
    M.B. July 17, 1787   Surety: George Stainback
    Consent: John Cardin, father of Jincy

TUCKER, Daniel, Jr.   Mary Parrish
    M.B. February 8, 1808   Surety: William Parrish

TUCKER, George   Eddy Short
    M.B. April 23, 1800   Surety: Daniel Tucker
    Minister: Charles Ogburn

TUCKER, Harwood B.   Nancy Mason
    M.B. January 9, 1809   Surety: William Stone

TUCKER, Isham   Rose Eaton
    M.B. February 2, 1786   Surety: James Bing

TUCKER, Isham   Sarah Booker
    M.B. May 11, 1803   Surety: William Renn
    Minister: William Creath

TUCKER, James P.   Catherine Tucker
    M.B. December 14, 1772   Surety: Robert Williams

TUCKER, James   Jane Tucker
    M.B. September 6, 1809   Surety: William Insco

TUCKER, James   Ruth Puckett
    M.B. May 17, 1810   Surety: G. B. Hudson

TUCKER, Jesse   Nancy Carroll
    M.B. November 7, 1793   Surety: John Carroll

TUCKER, John   Sally Nunnery
    M.B. January 22, 1793   M. January 25, 1793
    Minister: Charles Ogburn   Surety: Charnal Deardin

TUCKER, John   Frances Tucker
    M.B. December 10, 1798   M. December 28, 1798
    Minister: William Creath   Surety: Leonard Keeton

TUCKER, Littleberry   Elizabeth Kelly
    M.B. December 22, 1797   M. December 29, 1797
    Minister: Charles Ogburn   Surety: John Tucker

TUCKER, Robert   Sarah Smith
    M.B. November 12, 1787   Surety: Edward Elam

TUCKER, Tapla   Nancy Kelly
    M.B. December 9, 1799   Surety: Daniel Tucker
    Minister: William Creath

TUCKER, Worsham   Mary Gordon
    M.B. December 5, 1804   M. December 6, 1804
    Minister: Matthew Dance   Surety: John Gosee

TUDOR, John   Milly Spurlock
    M.B. July 16, 1786   Surety: Zachariah Spurlock

TURNER, Bailey   Susanna Easter
    M.B. December 1, 1792   M. December 20, 1792
    Minister: Edward Almand   Surety: John Oliver

TURNER, Drury   Tallathacuma Jackson
    M.B. December 11, 1802   Surety: Matthew Jackson

TURNER, John   Mary Hutcheson
    M.B. October 13, 1800   Surety: Aurelius Walker

TURNER, John   Rebeccah Taylor
    M.B. December 8, 1800   M. December 11, 1800
    Minister: James Meacham   Surety: James Taylor, Jr.

TURNER, Stephen   Martha Wright
    M.B. March 11, 1801   Surety: Austen Wright

TURNER, Terisha   * Joanah Reaves
    M.B. December 19, 1785   M. December 22, 1785
    Minister: John King   Surety: John Burton
    Consent: Stephen Turner, relation not stated
    Consent: Thomas Rives, relation not stated
    * Joanna Rives

TURNER, Thomas Weaver   Betty Merryman
    M.B. November 1, 1786   Surety: Isham Merryman
    Consent: James Turner, father of Thomas Weaver

VALENTINE, Buckner   Sine Chavous
    M.B. December 21, 1802   Surety: Bolling Chavous

VALENTINE, Charles   Nancy Chavous
    M.B. November 28, 1785   Surety: Thomas Macklin

VALENTINE, John   Mary McLin
    M.B. January 4, 1797   M. January 5, 1797
    Minister: John Loyd   Surety: Earby Chavous

VAUGHAN, Baalam   Polly Burnes
    M.B. December 11, 1809   M. December 12, 1809
    Minister: Richard Dabbs   Surety: Robert Burnes

VAUGHAN, Binns   Martha L. Arnold
    M.B. June 20, 1798   M. June 21, 1798
    Minister: Charles Ogburn   Surety: Thomas Edmundson

VAUGHAN, David   Patty Kirks
    M.B. August 3, 1803   Surety: John Hudgins

VAUGHAN, David   Philadelphia Griffin
    M.B. December 14, 1807   Surety: Hezekiah Yancey
    Consent: James Griffin, father of Philadelphia

VAUGHAN, Edmund H.   Sally H. Walker
    M.B. June 5, 1809   Surety: Francis E. Walker
    Minister: George Micklejohn

VAUGHAN, Henry G.   Nancy O. Wade
    M.B. January 3, 1803   M. January 5, 1803
    Minister: William Richards   Surety: William Wade

VAUGHAN, Ingram   Ann Lewis
    M.B. August 20, 1785   Surety: William Baskervill
    Consent: Edward Lewis, guardian of Ann Lewis and her
             brother

VAUGHAN, Ishmael   Caty Roberts
    M.B. October 24, 1797   Surety: William Roberts

VAUGHAN, Jairus   Hannah Vaughan
    M.B. July 11, 1796   M. August 3, 1796
    Minister: Charles Ogburn   Surety: Craddock Vaughan
    Consent: Richard Vaughan, father of Jairus
    Note: Hannah Pines Vaughan, daughter of Reuben and
          Elizabeth (Ingram) Vaughan

VAUGHAN, James   Judy Spain
    M.B. December 11, 1797   M. December 19, 1797
    Minister: William Richards   Surety: Sterling Spain
    Consent: Thomas Spain, father of Judith

VAUGHAN, James   Susannah Harris
    M.B. June 11, 1803   M. June 30, 1803
    Minister: William Richards   Surety: Richard Jeffries
    Consent: William Harris, father of Susannah

VAUGHAN, James   Mary Crow
     M.B. December 26, 1808   Surety: William Crow

VAUGHAN, John   Nancy Hayes
     M.B. December 13, 1802   Surety: Starky Hayes
     Minister: Baalam

VAUGHAN, Robert A.   Rebecca M. Davis
     M.B. January 4, 1806   Surety: Bushrod Webb
     Consent: Ambrose Vaughan, father of Robert
     Consent: Randolph Davis, father of Rebecca

VAUGHAN, Thomas   Ann Smith
     M.B. October 12, 1772   Surety: Swepson Jeffries

VAUGHAN, Thomas   Martha Lewis
     M.B. October 8, 1781   Surety: Edward Lewis

VAUGHAN, Thomas   Mary Alford Blackbourn
     M.B. March 11, 1799   Surety: John Wilson
     Note: Mary daughter of Thomas Blackbourn

VAUGHAN, William   Elizabeth Saunders
     M.B. March 3, 1794   M. March 6, 1794
     Minister: John Loyd   Surety: Ambrose Vaughan
     Consent: Richard Vaughan, father of William
     Consent: John Saunders, father of Elizabeth
     Note: Ambrose Vaughan of Brunswick County

VAUGHAN, William   Anne C. Gregory
     M.B. April 6, 1795   M. April 9, 1795
     Minister: Charles Ogburn   Surety: Richard Gregory

VAUGHAN, Woody   Sarah Farrar
     M.B. December 11, 1804   Surety: Sanford Bowers
     Consent: George Farrar, father of Sarah

VENABLE, Samuel   Ann Anderson
     M.B. March 5, 1782   Surety: Thomas Anderson
     Note: Samuel Venable of Prince Edward County
     Note: Ann, daughter of Thomas and Sarah Anderson

WADE, Henderson   Elizabeth Wilburn
     M.B. January 6, 1795   M. January 11, 1795
     Minister: William Richards   Surety: William Harrison

WADE, William   Martha Russell
     M.B. November 9, 1767   Surety: William Robertson

WADE, William   Polly Mealer Vaughan
    M.B. August 12, 179- *   August 15, 1799
    Minister: Edward Almand   Surety: Willis Vaughan
    * Year illegible, but minister's return says 1799

WAGSTAFF, Allen   Susannah Overton
    M.B. December 12, 1803   M. December 25, 1803
    Minister: William Richards   Sur: Philemon Hurt, Jr.

WAGSTAFF, Bazzell   Elizabeth Camp
    M.B. March 5, 1806   M. March 6, 1806
    Minister: William Richards   Surety: Allen Wagstaff

WAGSTAFF, Britain   Anne Freeman
    M.B. February 7, 1778   Surety: Allen Freeman
    Note: Anne, daughter of Allen Freeman

WALDEN, Eaton   Nanny Evans
    M.B. Decemver 20, 1788   Surety: Moses Stuart
    .Consent: Charles Evans, father of Nanny

WALDEN, Jarrel   Mourning Jackson
    M.B. September 16, 1801   Surety: John Harris

WALDEN, Jesse   Milly Stewart
    M.B. April 8, 1805   Surety: Frederick Ivey
    Minister: William Creath

WALDEN, John   Betsy Stewart
    M.B. April 21, 1804   Surety: Kinchen Chavous

WALKER, Aurelius   Nancy Turner
    M.B. November 23, 1784   Surety: William Allen
    Note: Nancy, daughter of Matthew Turner
    Note: Aurelius, son of Sylvanus Walker

WALKER, Daniel   Mary Brown
    M.B. August 5, 1793   Surety: Thomas Brown
    Note: Daniel Walker of Nottoway County

WALKER, Freeman   Polly Toone
    M.B. July 12, 1789   M. July 14, 1789
    Minister: John Williams   Surety: Lewis Toone

WALKER, George   Phebe Cheatham
    M.B. Dedember 14, 1789   Surety: Obadiah Cheatham
    Consent: Daniel Cheatham, father of Phebe who is
                 under age 18
    Note: George Hightower Walker, son of Sylvanus and
            Susannah Walker

WALKER, John   Anna Gregory
    M.B. November 12, 1798   M. November 15, 1798
    Minister: William Richards   Surety: Thomas Reamy

WALKER, Joseph R.   Dolly Winfield
    M.B. December 6, 1796   Surety: William Abernathy
    Consent: Joshua Winfield, father of Dolly

WALKER, Matthew   Rebecca Powers
    M.B. December 21, 1805   Surety: John Turner, Jr.

WALKER, Matthew   Sally Stone
    M.B. October 4, 1809   M. October 19, 1809
    Minister: Richard Dabbs   Surety: William Stone
    Note: Sally, daughter of William and Tabitha Stone
    Note: Matthew Walker, son of Aurelius and Nancy
        (Turner) Walker

WALKER, Richard H.   Nancy Vaughan
    M.B. July 10, 1798   Surety: Thomas Vaughan
    Note: Richard Henry Walker, son of Henry and Martha
        Bolling Walker

WALKER, William   Mary Bugg
    M.B. August 7, 1779   Surety: Henry Pennington
    Consent: John and Lucy Bugg, parents of Mary

WALL, Benjamin   Mary S. Bugg
    M.B. April 2, 1800   Surety: Frederick Wall
    Consent: Molly Bugg, mother of Mary

WALL, Burwell   Mary Burks
    M.B. September 30, 1794   Surety: Miles House
    Consent: Bride signs own consent and states that she
            is 25 years old

WALL, David S.   Rebecca J. Short
    M.B. July 3, 1805   Surety: George Stegall

WALL, Frederick   Patsy Wootton Daniel
    M.B. June 13, 1803   Surety: William Daniel

WALL, Henry   Sally Daniel
    M.B. December 17, 1810   Surety: Frederick Wall

WALL, John   Amey Hall
    M.B. December 10, 1787   Surety: James Hall
    Note: John Wall of Halifax County

WALL, John   Meloda Overby
    M.B. February 22, 1808   Surety: Peter Overby, Jr.
    Note: John Wall of Halifax County

WALL, Major   Mary James
    M.B. January 10, 1803   Surety: Frederick Poarch

WALL, Thomas   Elizabeth H. Short
    M.B. September 30, 1797   Surety: Freeman Short

WALL, Thomas   Jane Edmundson
    M.B. January 13, 1800   Surety: John Whobry
    Minister: William Creath

WALLACE, David   Nancy M. Wills
    M.B. March 22, 1798   March 24, 1798
    Minister: Charles Ogburn   Surety: Larkin Crowder

WALLER, Daniel   Frances Holmes
    M.B. April 29, 1788   Surety: John Waller
    Minister: Thomas Scott

WALLER, James   Susanna Wilson
    M.B. March 16, 1792   Surety: James Wilson
    Minister: John Loyd

WALLER, John   Ann Holmes
    M.B. March 5, 1782   Surety: John Ballard

WALLER, Starling   Rebecca Drumwright
    M.B. September 1, 1796   Surety: William Drumwright

WALTON, John   Dolly Ricks
    M.B. October 14, 1798   Surety: Richard Brown

WARREN, John   Betsy Holmes
    M.B. December 5, 1792   Surety: Walter Leigh
    Note: Betsy (Elizabeth), daughter of Samuel Holmes

WARREN, Marriott   Mary Holmes
    M.B. December 17, 1794   Surety: Benjamin Suggett
    Consent: Samuel Holmes, Sr., father of Mary
    Minister: John Neblett
    Note: Marriott Warren of Richmond County, Georgia

WARREN, William   Lucinda Holmes
    M.B. April 17, 1798   M. April 18, 1798
    Minister: Charles Ogburn   Surety: Samuel Holmes

WARTMAN, John Henry   Tabitha Epps
    M.B. November 24, 1787   Surety: Isham Epps

WATKINS, James   Ann Nuckols
    M.B. September 9, 1789   Surety: Philip Morgan

WATKINS, Thomas   Ellinor Farrar
    M.B. November 8, 1790   Surety: Thomas Farrar
    Minister: James Read

WATKINS, William Durham   Jane Bailey
    M.B. December 9, 1793   M. December 25, 1793
    Minister: William Creath   Surety: Henry Bailey

WATSON, James   Polly Jones Taylor
    M.B. January 27, 1796   M. January 28, 1796
    Minister: John Loyd   Surety: Abel Dortch

WATSON, James T.   Elizabeth Lark
    M.B. October 6, 1803   Surety: Samuel Lark, Sr.

WATSON, Thomas   Susanna Taylor
    M.B. December 27, 1791   Surety: William Poole
    Consent: Abel Dortch, relation not stated

WATTS, Richard   Lucy Collier
    M.B. March 10, 1806   Surety: William Lipford

WEATHERFORD, Freeman   Polly Smith
    M.B. December 8, 1800   Surety: Richard Thompson
    Consent: Buckner Smith, father of Polly
    Minister: William Creath

WEBB, Abdias   Patty Fain
    M.B. December 15, 1790   Surety: Frederick Rainey

WEBB, Bushrod   Catherine Lovingston
    M.B. January 7, 1800   M. January 8, 1800
    Minister: Ebenezer Macgowan   Surety: Mark L. Jackson

WEBB, John   Nancy Winn
    M.B. September 13, 1802   M. October 7, 1802
    Minister: William Richards   Surety: Littleberry Winn

WEBB, John   Sine Blankenship
    N. B. December 16, 1802   Surety: Mark L. Jackson

WEBSTER, Samuel   Charlotte Winkler
    M.B. August 1, 1788   Surety: Richardson Davis

WELLS, Baker   Levinia Underwood
    M.B. September 10, 1798   Surety: Zaccheus Ezell
    Minister: Matthew Dance   M. September 15, 1798

WELLS, David   Nancy Garrott
    M.B. October 11, 1799   Surety: Elijah Wells
    Consent: Thomas Garrott, father of Nancy
    Minister: William Creath

WELLS, Elijah   Sarah Ferrell
    M.B. September 14, 1795   Surety: John Hudson

WESTBROOK, Jesse   Amy Weatherford
    M.B. December 9, 1805   Surety: James Baker

WESTBROOK, Randolph   * Happy Sally
    M.B. December 10, 1798   M. December 26, 1798
    Minister: William Creath   Surety: John Allgood
    * Kerrenhappuck Salle'

WESTBROOK, Thomas   Sally Burrus
    M.B. December 9, 1805   M. December 24, 1805
    Minister: Edward Almand   Surety: Jesse Westbrook

WESTMORELAND, Robert   Polly Pennington
    M.B. December 5, 1804   Surety: George Tucker

WHITE, Henry   * Rebecca Overby
    M.B. December 21, 1805   Surety: Robert Davis
    Consent: Edward Delony, guardian gives consent for
            Henry White to marry Rebecca Overby
    * Marriage bond says "Rebecca Davis"

WHITE, James   Mary Greenwood
    M.B. February 28, 1786   M. March 12, 1786
    Minister: John Marshall   Surety: William Willis
    Consent: Thomas Greenwood, guardian of Mary

WHITE, John   Nancy Baker
    M.B. March 12, 1787   Surety: Thomas Feild
    Note: Nancy (Maryanna) Baker, daughter of Zachariah
            and Jane Baker

WHITE, John   Nancy Holloway
    M.B. December 12, 1797   M. December 14, 1797
    Minister: Edward Almand   Surety: Edward Holloway

WHITE, Larkin   Nelly Dedman
    M.B. December 9, 1793   Surety: Henry Dedman

WHITE, Robert   Jane Winn
    M.B. December 5, 1807   M. December 10, 1807
    Minister: William Richards   Surety: John Dedman

WHITE, William   Frances Greenwood
    M.B. June 21, 1791   M. July 20, 1791
    Minister: James Read   Surety: John Greenwood
    Consent: Thomas Greenwood, guardian of Frances

WHITLOW, James, Sr.   Penelope Hogwood
    M.B. May 18, 1803   Surety: John Bilbo

WHITLOW, William, Jr.   Mary Saunders
    M.B. October 12, 1795   M. October 17, 1795
    Minister: William Richards   Surety: Charles Burton

WHITWORTH, Samuel   Mary Hubbard Walden
    M.B. March 9, 1778   Surety: Peter Burton
    Note: Peter Burton states that Mary is 21 years old

WHOBRY, John *   Sarah Bugg
    M.B. March 6, 1794   M. March 9, 1794
    Minister: William Creath   Surety: John Bugg
    * Name spelled "Hoobry" also

WILBURN, Julius   Lucy Puryear
    M.B. March 15, 1798   Surety: William Vowell
    Consent: Thomas Puryear, father of Lucy
    Minister: William Creath

WILBURN, Thomas   Phebe Moore
    M.B. July 11, 1806   Surety: William Jones
    Consent: George Moore, father of Phebe

WILBURN, William   Patty Avery
    M.B. February 28, 1782   Surety: James Harrison

WILBURN, William   Elizabeth Hudson
    M.B. January 28, 1793   M. January 30, 1793
    Minister: Edward Almand   Surety: William Hudson

WILES, Mastin   Claresy Epperson
    M.B. September 13, 1802   M. October 16, 1802
    Minister: Baalam Ezell   Surety: Joseph Epperson

WILKINS, Charles   Elizabeth Puryear
    M.B. June 22, 1795   Surety: John Farrar
    Minister: William Creath
    Note: Charles Wilkins of Rutherford County, N. C.

WILLIAMS, David   Milly Newton
    M.B. June 11, 1804   Surety: John Williams

WILLIAMS, James   Mary Durham
    M.B. May 8, 1797   M. May 17, 1797
    Minister: William Richards   Surety: Eusebius Stone

WILLIAMS, Jeremiah   Dolly Carter
    M.B. November 27, 1802   M. December 1, 1802
    Minister: Edward Almand   Surety: Joseph N. Meredith

WILLIAMS, John   Elizabeth Taylor
    M.B. October 26, 1791   M. October 27, 1791
    Minister: John Loyd   Surety: Samuel Holmes, Jr.

WILLIAMS, Leroy   Amey Mills
    M.B. December 24, 1794   M. December 27, 1794
    Minister: Charles Ogburn   Surety: George Baker
    Consent: Susanna Stubbs, mother of Amey

WILLIAMS, Thomas   Sally Alderson
    M.B. July 27, 1808   Surety: Robert Garrott

WILLIAMS, William   Judith Baker
    M.B. January 8, 1796   M. February 11, 1796
    Minister: William Creath   George Baker

WILLIAMSON, John   Susanna Yancey
    M.B. September 3, 1802   M. September 4, 1802
    Minister: Baalam Ezell   Surety: Richard Murray
    Consent: Robert Yancey, father of Susanna

WILLIAMSON, Merryman   Sally Thomason
    M.B. July 29, 1803   Surety: Archibald Merryman

WILLIAMSON, Robert   Mary Yancey
    M.B. January 25, 1793   M. January 31, 1793
    Minister: James Read   Surety: William Baskervill

WILLIS, Edward   Polly Moore
    M.B. December 21, 1801   Surety: James Browder

WILLIS, James   Lucy Nash
    M.B. November 14, 1783   Surety: John Crews

WILLIS, John   Sally Pulliam
    M.B. December 10, 1792   M. December 15, 1792
    Minister: James Read   Surety: Richard Carter

WILLIS, William   Lucy Moore
    M.B. April 16, 1782   Surety: James Willis

WILLS, Robert   Jane Colley
    M.B. October 13, 1788   Surety: Edward Colley

WILSON, Archibald   Martha Bevill
    M.B. October 26, 1785   Surety: Hutchins Burton

WILSON, Caleb   Elizabeth Ballard
    M.B. January 5, 1803   Surety: Francis Ballard
    Note: Caleb Wilson of Orange County, N. C.

WILSON, Daniel   Elizabeth Cheatham
    M.B. August 28, 1778   William Waddill
    Consent: Leonard Cheatham, father of Elizabeth

WILSON, Henry   Caty Waller
    M.B. June 25, 1790   Surety: Daniel Waller

WILSON, John, Jr.   Elizabeth Smith
    M.B. September 12, 1791   Surety: Thomas Burnett
    Consent: Joseph Townes, guardian of Elizabeth

WILSON, John   Nancy Goodwin
    M.B. January 2, 1793   Surety; Robert Baskervill

WILSON, Miles   Margaret Feild
    M.B. February 13, 1809   Surety: Erasmus Kennon
    Consent: Jane Feild, mother of Margaret
    Minister: George Micklejohn

WILSON, Robert   Eleanor Dedman
    M.B. June 9, 1794   M. June 13, 1794
    Minister: John Williams   Surety: Larkin White

WILSON, Robert   Hannah Stone
    M.B. May 9, 1808   M. May 18, 1808
    Minister: Richard Dabbs   Surety: William Stone
    Note: Hannah, daughter of William and Tabitha Stone

WILSON, Thomas   Elizabeth Vaughan
    M.B. November 10, 1789   Surety: Robert Birtchett
    Minister: Thomas Scott

WILSON, William   Rebecca Brown
    M.B. September 9, 1782   Surety: Thomas Brown

WINFIELD, Arthur Freeman   Susannah Courtney
    M.B. June 2, 1786   Surety: Samuel Holmes
    Note: Susannah, daughter of Clack and Prudence
          Courtney

WINFIELD, Joel   Polly Booth
    M.B. March 3, 1801   M. March 4, 1801
    Minister: James Meacham   Surety: Joshua Winfield

WINN, Banister   Nancy Naish
    M.B. December 11, 1809   M. December 12, 1809
    Minister: William Richards   Surety: Benjamin Blake

WINN, Harrison   Frances Haile
    M.B. July 11, 1785   Surety: Thomas Haile

WINN, Littleberry   Mary Maynard
    M.B. December 29, 1783   Surety: William Maynard

WINN, Richard   Sarah Hall
    M.B. August 14, 1775   Surety: James Hall

WOODSON, Miller, Jr.   Sophia W. Hendrick
    M.B. August 8, 1803   Surety: Amasa Palmer

WOODSON, Tscharner   Lucy Michaux
    M.B. September 8, 1788   Surety: William Hendrick
    Consent: Joseph Michaux, guardian of Lucy

WOOTTON, John   Mary Christopher
    M.B. March 18, 1785   Surety: William Daniel
    Note: Mary, daughter of David Christopher, deceased

WOOTTON, Samuel   Martha Hyde
    M.B. November 10, 1788   M. November 27, 1788
    Minister: Thomas Scott   Surety: John Hyde
    Note: Martha, daughter of John Hyde, Senr.

WORSHAM, John   Lucy Hamblin
    M.B. November 12, 1804   Surety: Stephen P'Pool

WORSHAM, Stephen   Nancy Blanks
    M.B. September 14, 1807   Surety: Daniel Jones

WORTHAM, James   Jincy McQuie
    M.B. November 11, 1799   Surety: Thomas A. Jones

WRIGHT, Anderson   Phebe Malone Watson
    M.B. May 27, 1793   M. May 30, 1793
    Minister: John Loyd   Surety: William Poole, Jr.

WRIGHT, Anderson   Elizabeth Langford
    M.B. December 6, 1794   M. December 11, 1794
    Minister: John Loyd   Surety: James Watson

WRIGHT, Austin, Senr.   Lucy Holloway
    M.B. March 1, 1806   Surety: Francis Ballard

WRIGHT, Bolling   Milly Saunders
    M.B. July 30, 1787   Surety: John Feagins
    Consent: John Saunders, father of Milly

WRIGHT, Claiborne   Patsy Nanney
    M.B. December 27, 1792   M. December 29, 1792
    Minister: John Loyd   Surety: Hughberry Nanney

WRIGHT, David   Nancy Wright
    M.B. December 28, 1797   Surety: Roderick Wright
    Note: David Wright of Lunenburg County

WRIGHT, James   Sarah Easter
    M.B. December 23, 1784   Surety: Leonard Smith

WRIGHT, John   Sarah Fox
    M.B. October 3, 1797   Surety: William Taylor
    Consent: Richard Fox, father of Sarah

WRIGHT, John   Sally Holmes
    M.B. May 13, 1801   M. May 21, 1801
    Minister: Ebenezer Macgowan   Surety: John Holmes

WRIGHT, John   Rebecca Oslin
    M.B. June 19, 1802   Surety: Isaac Oslin

WRIGHT, Robert   Nancy Wright
    M.B. November 16, 1792   Surety: Austin Wright
    Note: Robert Wright of Brunswick County

WRIGHT, Roderick   Martha Cleaton
    M.B. September 19, 1795   M. September 24, 1795
    Minister: John Loyd   Surety: Thomas Cleaton, Jr.

WRIGHT, Sterling   Silviah Davis
    M.B. July 4, 1788   Surety: Josiah Floyd

WRIGHT, William   Nancy Palmer
    M.B. December 12, 1804   Surety: Thomas Wright

WYATT, Walter   Elizabeth Brame
    M.B. December 16, 1792   Surety: James Brame

YANCEY, Hezekiah   Sally Worsham
    M.B. October 10, 1808   Surety: John Williamson

YANCEY, Jechonias   Rebecca L. Royster
    M.B. December 15, 1788   Surety: George Royster

YANCEY, John   Mary Hamblin
    M.B. October 14, 1799   Surety: Daniel Jones
    Consent: Thomas Hamblin, father of Mary
    Minister: William Creath

YANCEY, Minge   Frances Knott
    M.B. May 9, 1808   Surety: Samuel C. Brame

YANCEY, Robert   Agnes Wilkerson
    M.B. October 11, 1796   Surety: Francis Griffin

YATES, Edward Randolph   Elizabeth Murray
    M.B. September 20, 1783   Surety: Asa Oliver
    Consent: William Yates, guardian of Edward R.
    Note: Elizabeth, daughter of John Murray

YOUNG, Allen   Sarah Davis
    M.B. May 22, 1779   Surety: Samuel Young
    Note: Sarah, daughter of William Davis

YOUNG, Coleman   Mary Standley
    M.B. December 18, 1788   Surety: James Standley

YOUNG, John   Jane Swepson
    M.B. January 24, 1784   Surety: Enos Easter

INDEX

ABERNATHY
 Lucy 38
 Martha 99
ADAMS
 Lizzy 33
 Lucy 9, 48
 Mary 112
 Rebecca 38
 _____ 109
ALDERSON
 Sally 133
ALEXANDER
 Martha 99
ALLEN
 Anne 12
 Elizabeth 65, 115
 Judith 115
 Leanna 105
 Margaret 85
 Nancy 111
 Polly 49
 Rebecca 11
 Sally 7
 Susanna 103
ALLGOOD
 Betsy H. 84
 Dicy 67
 Elizabeth 16, 30, 31
 Judith 58
 Lucy 34
 Nancy 76
 Sarah 69
ALVIS
 Betsy 30
AMBROSE
 Mary 120
ANDERSON
 Ann 126
 Henryetta Maria 46
 Lucy 64
 Mary 81
 Sarah 75
 Susannah 81
ANDREWS
 Anne 10, 22
 Betsy 50
 Elizabeth 50
 Martha W. 23
 Nancy 118
 Polly 116

APPERSON
 Lucy 108
 Martha 46
 Polly 54
ARNOLD
 Amy 47
 Betty 33
 Jane 78
 Lucy 107
 Martha L. 125
 Milly 42
 Patty 82
 Polly 20
ATKINS
 Jilley 108
ATKINSON
 Ann 42
 Median 42
AVERETT
 Louise 81
AWARY
 Elizabeth M. 113
AVERY
 Lockey 51
 Patty 132
AVORY
 Elizabeth 55
 Fanny 70

BAILEY
 Dolly 47
 Elizabeth 95
 Jane 130
 Martha 86
 Nancy 36
 Prissey 57
 Sarah 20
BAIRD
 Betsy 97
BAKER
 Ann 94
 Jincy 88
 Judith 133
 Maryanna 65
 Nancy 131
 Sarah 12
BALLARD
 Elizabeth 133

BALLARD
  Martha Elizabeth 96
  Mary Garland 80
  Rebecca 39
BAPTIST
  Elizabeth L. 85
  Mary 87
  Matilda 32
BARNETT
  Becky 45
  Martha C. 119
BARRY
  Margaret 60
  Peggy 86
BASKERVILL
  Ann 46
  Elizabeth 75
  Martha 82
  Mary 96
  Susanna 46
BASS
  Sylvia 12
BAUGH
  Agnes 7
  Elizabeth 112
  Frances 83
  Martha 60
  Sarah 69
  Tabitha 63
BEASLEY
  Nancy 30
BECKLEY
  Mary Ann 54
BEDDINGFIELD
  Susanna 116
BENFORD
  Polly 103
  Sally 120
BENTLY
  Ann 101
BERRY
  Molly 67
  Sarah 59
BEVILL
  Elizabeth 64
  Martha 133
  Micah 31
BIGNAL
  Sarah 31
BILBO
  Agnes 90
  Elizabeth 22
  Martha Minge 14

BILBO
  Mary 90
  Susannah 84
  Susanna 111
BILLUPS
  Lucy R. 84
BING
  Elizabeth 77
  Nancy 76
BIRTCHETT
  Elenor H. 115
  Elizabeth 81
  Martha 52
BISHOP
  Barsheba 103
BLACKBOURN
  Lucy Charlotte 66
  Mary Alford 126
BLACKETTER
  Elizabeth B. 9
  Keziah 74
  Nancy 56
  Polly 118
BLAIR
  Sally 28
BLAKE
  Jinsey 9
BLAND
  Betsy 21
  Fanny 68
BLANKENSHIP
  Jemima 63
  Sine 130
BLANKS
  Dycy 56
  Edna 54
  Nancy 135
BLANTON
  Elizabeth 117
  Sally 165
BOOKER
  Sarah 123
BOOTH
  Judith 75
  Lucy Gillam 58
  Nancy 74
  Polly 134
BOOTHE
  Rebecca 44
  Susannah 47
BOSWELL
  Ermin 40

BOTTOM
    Nancy 105
    Sarah 79
BOWEN
    Caty 83
    Charlotte 17
    Judy 17
    Liza 83
    Lucy 55
    Milly 36
    Nancy 107
    Omea 18
    Rebecca 72
    Stacy 26
BOYD
    Elizabeth 46
    Jane A. 61
    Nancy 61
BOZWELL
    Martha 17
BRADLEY
    Elizabeth 56
BRAME
    Elizabeth 30, 136
    Elizabeth R. 24
    Hannah C. 70
    Happy 49
    Lucy 35
    Mary 113
    Susannah 30
    Susanna 82, 19
BRANDON
    Elizabeth 33
    Mary 51
    Nancy 52
BRAWNER
    Mary 8
BRIGGS
    Elizabeth 38
BROADFOOT
    Margaret 10
BROGDON
    Molly Harris 48
BROOK
    Elizabeth 97
    Sarah 84
BROOKE
    Mary 57
BROOKING
    Lucy 63
BROOKS
    Elizabeth 56

BROOKS
    Jincy 79
    Lucy 14
    Molly 24
    Nelly 74
BROWN
    Amy W. 70
    Anne 12
    Catherine 11
    Elizabeth 94
    Hannah H. 82
    Martha 71
    Mary 119, 127
    Olive 114
    Rebecca 134
    Sally 34
BRUMMELL
    Polly 35
BUGG
    Ann 81
    Betty 66
    Elizabeth 8, 38
    Frances 92
    Joyce 79
    Lucy 7, 50
    Martha 96
    Mary 128
    Mary S. 128
    Nancy 71
    Rebecca 48
    Sarah 64, 80, 132
BURKS
    Mary 128
BURNES
    Polly 125
BURNETT
    Elizabeth 114
    Nancy 121
    Polly Jeffries 80
    Sally 16, 63
BURROWS
    Elizabeth 107
BURRUS
    Amasa 106
    Elizabeth 15, 24
    Rebecca 34
    Sally 131
BURTON
    Dolly 114
    Frances 64
    Martha 14
    Mary 47, 80, 98

BURTON
    Miney   106
    Peggy M.   71
    Phebe   102, 104
    Susanna   41
BURWELL
    Anne Spottswood   104
    Christian   57
    Elizabeth Blair   118
    Frances Powell   78
    Mary   110
    Mary Armistead   52
    Matilda   18
    Panthea   18
BUTLER
    Charlotte   81
    Elizabeth D.   57
    Mary   15
    Nancy   121
    Patsy   58
    Sarah   74

CAMP
    Elizabeth   127
    Mary   66
CAMPBELL
    Susanna   86
CARDIN
    Jincy   123
CARLESS
    Frances H.   120
CARLETON
    Rebecca   103
    Susanna   34
CARROLL
    Jinney   24
    Judith   7
    Martha   33
    Mourning   60
    Nancy   123
CARTER
    Caty   20
    Dolly   132
    Judy   77
    Patsy   55
    Polly   93
    Sally   73, 35
    Susanna   110
CATTILER
    Sary   116

CHAMBERLAIN
    Elizabeth   24, 95
    Sarah   90
CHAMBERS
    Betsy   93
CHAMBLISS
    Mary   79
CHANDLER
    Jean   116
CHAPPELL
    Amey   51
CHAVOUS
    Anna   55
    Elizabeth 20, 110
    Jincy   116
    Lydia   58
    Milly   28
    Nancy   124
    Ryte   117
    Sine   124
    Suckee   51
CHEATHAM
    Betsy   115
    Elizabeth   133
    Mary   39
    Phebe   127
    Sarah   76
CHILDERS
    Sally   45
CHILDRESS
    Elizabeth   96
    Jean   57
CHRISTOPHER
    Elizabeth   47
    Frances   84
    Hannah   81
    Mary   135
    Nancy   100, 57
    Sally   68
    Susannah   96
CLANCH
    Sally   27
CLARK
    Dianna   19
    Elizabeth 65, 81
    Mary   37
    Nancy   122
    Sarah   46
    Susanna   75
CLARKE
    Polly   7

CLAUNCH
Jinny 9
CLAUSEL
Aphia W. 12
Frances 102
Hannah H. 20
Lucy 36
Martha 102
Sally S. 102
CLAY
Judith 42
Patience 99
Prudence 82
Rebecca 47
Temperance 44, 16
CLEATON
Edith 101
Elizabeth 92
Jincy 78
Martha 136
CLEMONDS
Mary 15
COLE
Jincy 34
Nancy 91
Sukey 51
COLEMAN
Ann 53
Elizabeth 72, 112
Elizabeth C. 94
Gracey 63
Jane 91
Jane S. 74
Martha 109
Mary 17
Polly A. 115
Rebeccah 99
Sally 30
COLLEY
Agness 55
Elizabeth 16
Jane 133
Martha 8
COLLIER
Lucy 130
Sarah 47, 70
Susannah B. 105
COMER
Frances 8
COOK
Elizabeth 79
Happy 119

COOK
Martha 104
Polly 93
COOPER
Nancy 8
Rebecca 28
COPPEDGE
Elizabeth 85
Susanna 120
CORN
Keziah 117
COUCH
Letty 54
COURTNEY
Ann C. 84
Prudence 65
Susannah 134
COX
Frances 117
Francinia 53
Letitia 44
Lucretia 86
Mary F. 16
Nancy 56
Patsey 8
Phebe 17
Rebecca 91
Sarah 57, 60, 73
Susanna 101
Talitha 21
CRAWLEY
Elizabeth 53
Lucy 24
CREEDLE
Elizabeth 118
Hannah 33
CRENSHAW
Mary 75
Nancy 86
Rachel 74

CREW
Delia 11
Parthena 74
CREWS
Nancy 106
Susannah 62
CROOK
Rebeccah 112
CROW
Lucy 56
Mary 126

143

CROWDER
    Amey   26
    Angelina   100
    Anne   23
    Betsy   65
    Cary   85
    Delilah   77
    Elizabeth   78, 92
    Frances   65, 77
    Levisy   104
    Libelar   41
    Linchey   73
    Lytha   41
    Martha   95
    Mary   25, 26, 62, 78
    Milly   23
    Obedience   11
    Patsy   110
    Rebecca   23
CRUTCHFIELD
    Lucy   120
    Martha   59
CULBREATH
    Elizabeth   27
    Lucy   62
    Margaret   89
    Polly   37
CUNNINGHAM
    Sally   12
CURTIS
    Betsy   49
    Elizabeth   71
    Jessie   11
    Lucy   118

DAILEY
    Susanna   44
DALY
    Ann   94, 112
    Betsy   7
    Elizabeth B.   19
    Elizabeth H.   50
    Frances   121
    Sarah   95
DANIEL
    Luritta   29
    Milly   122, 56
    Patsy Wootton   128
    Polly   38
    Sally   128

DAVIS
    Elizabeth   39, 119
    Hannah   27
    Jane H.   9
    Jane J.   74
    Janey   42
    Lucy   61
    Nancy   28
    Polly   79, 122
    Rebecca   131
    Rebecca M.   126
    Sally   96
    Sarah   22, 136
    Silviah   136
    Susanna   15
DAWS
    Lucy   32
    Martha   31
    Rebecca   65
DECKER
    Catey   61
DEDMAN
    Eleanor   134
    Nelly   131
DELONY
    Francis   63
    Lucy   20
    Mary   97
DENNIS
    Lurita   28
DODSON
    Ann   107
    Elizabeth   68
    Polly   107
DOGGETT
    Mary   79
    Sarah   54
DORTCH
    Ann   47
    Helina   91
    Lucy   109
    Rebecca   119
DOUGLAS
    Elizabeth   21, 83
    Martha   27
DRAPER
    Elizabeth   108
    Frances   108
    Mary   34
    Sarah   67
DREW
    Elizabeth   116

DREW
     Nancy   55
     Precilla   28
DRUMMOND
     Mavel   18
     Nancy   37
DRUMWRIGHT
     Frances   10
     Lucy   91
     Martha   69
     Nancy   119
     Rebecca   129
     Sally   91
DUPREY
     Jane   38
DURHAM
     Mary   132
     Nancy   72
     Patsy   11
     .Sarah   66

EASTER
     Margaret   10
     Martha   35
     Sarah   135
     Susanna   124
EASTHAM
     Dicy   82
EASTLAND
     Elizabeth   82
     Mary   7
EATON
     Nancy   7
     Rose   123
EDDINS
     Lucy   49
EDMONDSON
     Martha   10
EDMUNDSON
     Anne   57
     Elizabeth   108
     Jane   129
     Rachel   99
EDWARDS
     Elizabeth   26
     Martha   35
     Polly   11
ELAM
     Elizabeth   43, 51
     Frances   53

ELAM
     Labia   54
     Martha   55
     Mary   49, 82
     Mary I.   59
     Nancy   60
     Phebe   90
     Sarah   116
ELLIOTT
     Jinny   25
ELLIS
     Patsy   37, 100
     Sally   113
     Sarah   48
EMERY
     Hally   109
EPPERSON
     Celey   71
     Claresy   132
     Elizabeth   48
     Fanny   26
EPPES
     Elizabeth   92
     Martha   111
EPPS
     Tabitha   129
ERBY
     Nancy   55
ERSKINE
     Mary C.   66
EVANS
     Catharine   104
     Delilah   83
     Elizabeth   84, 111
     Martha   45
     Mary   105
     Nancy   71
     Nanny   127
     Polly   27
     Prudence   83
     Rebeccah   85
     Sally   66
EZELL
     Martha   50
     Rebecca   67

FAIN
     Patty   130
FARGESON
     Martha   48

FARRAR
    Elizabeth 47
    Ellinor 129
    Martha 15, 29
    Nancy 65
    Sarah 46, 126
FEAGINS
    Lisha 101
FEILD
    Margaret 134
FERGUSON
    Sarah 58
FERRELL
    Elizabeth T. 40
    Martha 118
    Sarah 130
FIELD
    Jane 66
FINCH
    Frances 98
    Phebe 111
    Polly 17
    Susanna 16
FINN
    Jincy 18
    Prudence 91
    Sally 85
FLOYD
    Patty 98
    Phebey 39
FOSTER
    Catherine 24
FOWLER
    Dolly 104
FOWLKES
    Nancy 96
    Sarah 84
FOX
    Hannah 65
    Mary 83
    Nancy 103
    Priscilla 119
    Sally 95
    Sarah 135
FRAZER
    Elizabeth 52
FREEMAN
    Anne 127
    Jane 21
    Mary 122

GARNER
    Martha 43

GARNER
    Polly W. 43
    Susannah 62
    Winny 122
GARROTT
    Mary 71
    Nancy 130
GEE
    Lucy 41
    Nancy 50
GILES
    Elizabeth 92, 100
    Jane Perrin 13
GILLIAM
    Martha 78
GILLESPIE
    Susanna 64
GLOVER
    Nancy 83
    Sally 107
GOBER
    Molly 120
GOLD
    Elizabeth 56
    Milly 122
GOODE
    Elizabeth 60
    Elizabeth Willis 119
    Isabell 72
    Jane 100
    Mary 48
    Nancy 67
    Rebecca 111
GOODWIN
    Lucy 67
    Nancy 134
    Susanna 19
GORDON
    Ann 64
    Jincy 63
    Mary 124
    Peggy 23
GRAVES
    Elizabeth 52, 59
    Fanny W. 60
    Lucretia 27
    Nancy 47
    Sally 116
GREEN
    Elizabeth 95
    Mary 123
    Patsy 61
    Polly 26
    Sarah 48

GREEN
    Sally 93
GREENWOOD
    Ann 62
    Avarilla 109
    Elizabeth 62
    Frances 131
    Jane 96
    Mary 131
    Sally 80
GREER
    Jane 15
GREFFIES
    Sally 26
GREGORY
    Anna 128
    Anne 81
    Anne C. 126
    Elizabeth 79, 116
    Fanny D. 12
    Frances 25
    Martha 107
    Mary 21
    Mary C. 120
    Patsy 80
    Sarah 33, 61
    Susanna 43
GRIFFIN
    Elizabeth 117
    Margaret 117
    Mary 46
    Nancy 40
    Philadelphia 125
    Susanna 54
GRIGG
    Betsy 31
    Patsy 92
    Sally 105
GWALTNEY
    Susanna 112
GUY
    Elizabeth 75
    Fanny 84

HAILE
    Frances 134
    Mary 27
HAILESTOCK
    Mary 121

HAILEY
    Dosha 75
    Jane 51
HALL
    Amey 128
    Anne 65
    Martha B. 34
    Sarah 134
    Susanna 108
HALTON
    Prudence 60
HAMBLIN
    Elizabeth 86, 122
    Lucy 135
    Martha Cocke 120
    Mary 136
    Nancy 75
    Phebe 45
    Rebeccah 23
HAMLIN
    Martha 74
HANSERD
    Mary 99
    Sarah 110
HARDY
    Jane B. 44
    Martha, Widow 94
HARPER
    Frances 85
    Martha 17
HARRIS
    Dicey 9
    Judith 115
    Mary 52
    Nanny 30
    Patsy 102
    Rebekah 109
    Sally 30, 96
    Susanna 58
    Susannah 125
HARRISON
    Elizabeth 73, 112
    Nancy 90
    Winny 104
HARWELL
    Elizabeth P. 14
    Martha 60
HASKINS
    Ann N. 20
    Elizabeth 32, 115

HASTEN
    Lively 36
HATCH
    Martha 33
HATCHELL
    Sally 17
HATSELL
    Elizabeth 57
    Frances 95
    Polly 57
    Polly Lewis 34
    Sally Hunt 101
HAWKINS
    Sarah 100
HAYES
    Kitty 102
    Mary 104
    Nancy 126
HEATHCOCK
    Honora 116
HENDRICK
    Judith 96
    Leah 12
    Permelia B. 52
    Sophia W. 134
HENLY
    Martha 110
HESTER
    Ann 101
    Anna 83, 89
    Barbara 19, 20
    Elizabeth 81
    Henrietta 53
    Jane 19, 85
    Lilly 19
    Lucy 21
    Martha 97
    Mary 24, 89
HICKS
    Duannar 11
HIGHTOWER
    Sarah 14
HILL
    Phebe 61
HINTON
    Mary 100
    Nancy 100
HIX
    Elizabeth 62
    Lucy 22
HOBSON
    Agness 43

HOGAN
    Ann 72
    Ede 45
    Mary 44
    Prudence 108
HOGWOOD
    Penelope 131
HOLLINS
    Caty 9
HOLLOWAY
    Dianna 34
    Elizabeth 47, 120
    Lucy 135
    Martha 12
    Nancy 131
    Patsy 68
    Sally 87
HOLMES
    Ann 68, 129
    Betsy 129
    Elizabeth 38, 74
    Faithy 114
    Fanny 22
    Frances 129
    Joice 51
    Lucinda 129
    Lucy 118
    Martha 7
    Mary 40, 129
    Mary A. 44
    Patty 80
    Polly 12
    Rebecca 103
    Sally 105, 135
    Sarah 39
    Susannah 13
HOOD
    Keziah 43
HOPKINS
    Elizabeth 39
    Jane 101
HORD
    Fanny 87
HOUSE
    Nancy 37
HOWARD
    Martha 91
HUBBARD
    Patsy 114
HUDGINS
    Dolly 42
    Elizabeth F. 107

HUDSON
    Betty 69
    Clary   59
    Dicey   9
    Elizabeth 9, 25, 132
    Judith   103
    Lucy   49, 100
    Margary   34
    Nancy   26
    Polly   102
    Sarah   89
    Susanna   104
HUMPHRIES
    Caty   26
    Martha   24
    Monica   23
    Nancy   87
    Stacy   10
HUNDLEY
    Lucy   122
    Nancy   117
    Polly   44
HUNT
    Elizabeth   52
    Lockey   26
    Mary Ann   62
    Nancy   46
HURT
    Ann   74
    Patience   43
HUTCHESON
    Anna   19
    Elizabeth   14, 44
    Elizabeth   97, 117
    Elizabeth C.   77
    Fanny   68
    Frances C.   25
    Hannah   90
    Lucy   112
    Martha   99
    Mary   124
    Polly   72
    Sally   21
    Sarah   69
    Susanna   63, 117
HUTSON
    Sarah 21
HUTT
    Jincy   64
    Letty   107
    Mary   105
    Nancy   35
    Sally   34
    Leliah   93

HYDE
    Elinor   113
    Martha   135
    Sarah   43

INGE
    Sally   31
INGRAM
    Lucy   105
    Lucy Worsham   25
    Martha   98
    Tabitha   122
INSCO
    Jinny   29
    Martha N.   14

JACKSON
    Betsy Ann 75
    Charity 75
    Elizabeth   47
    Jemima   79
    Mourning   127
    Nancy   121
    Prudence   30
    Sally   14
    Sarah   75
    Tallathacuma   124
JAMES
    Mary   129
JEFFRIES
    Ann   95
    Elizabeth 23, 72, 95
    Jane   12, 94
    Lucy   21
    Martha   23, 44
    Nancy   49
    Polly Cluverius 21
    Sarah   22
    Susannah   64
    Susannah B.   36
JOHNSON
    Betsy 37
    Caty   28
    Frances   112
    Jane   89
    Leannah   44
    Martha   86
    Nancy   41
    Rebecca   37
    Sarah   70

149

LOCKETT
  Anne   51
  Elizabeth   16
  Lucy   76
  Nancy   62
  Phebe   98
LOVE
  Agnes   106
LOVINGSTON
  Catherine   130
LOWRY
  Polly   49
LOYD
  Celia   91
  Martha   35
  Rebekah   36
LUCAS
  Ann   41
  Elizabeth W.   40
  Frances   63
  Sarah   96
  Susanna P.   97
LUNSFORD
  Polly   44

McDANIEL
  Lucy   118
McHARG
  Elizabeth Q.   7
  Mary Watts   62
McKINNEY
  Jinny   38
McLAUGHLIN
  Elizabeth   108
McLIN
  Fanny   28
  Mary   125
McQUIE
  Jincy   135

MABRY
  Angelica   50
  Elizabeth   17
  Polly   98
MALLETT
  Elizabeth   85
MALONE
  Betsy   110

MALONE
  Lizzy   111
  Lucy   30
  Patsy   55
  Sally   92
  Sophia   56
           88
MANNING
  Polly   116
MARKS
  Nancy   87
MARRIOTT
  Constant   8
MARSHALL
  Alice   37
  Ann   122
  Betsy Green   73
  Elizabeth   63, 102
  Martha Goode   82
  Mary Ann   14
  Nancy   111
  Phibby A.   34
  Sally   37
  Sally Read   17
  Susanna   56
  Susannah   13
MASON
  Lucy   76
  Milly   45
  Nancy   123
  Patsy   35
  Rebecca   105
  Rody   83
MASSEY
  Betsy   44
  Mary   13
MATTHEWS
  Elizabeth   32
  Martha   89, 115
  Nancy   100
  Sarah   59
MAY
  Siller   105
MAYES
  Elizabeth   45, 56
MAYNARD
  Frances   14
  Judith   51
  Mary   134
MAYNE
  Mary M.   31
  Parmelia   73

MAYNE
    Patsy M. 79
MEALER
    Elizabeth 116
    Frances 103
    Martha   101
    Susanna   103
MEDLEY
    Lucy   46
MERRYMAN
    Betty 124
    Polly   78
    Sally 13
MICHAUX
    Lucy 134
MILLS
    Amey 132
MINOR
    Betsy 36
    Sarah 72
MITCHELL
    Nancy 21
    Patsey 24
    Rebeccah 22
MONROE
    Polly 37
MOODY
    Elizabeth 90
    Mary   38
    Nancy   54
    Phebe 119
    Polly   89
MOORE
    Betsy 76
    Elizabeth 94
    Lucy 133
    Martha   51
    Mary   37
    Mary Anne 109
    Phebe   132
    Polly   133
    Rebeccah 122
    Taffanus   68
MORGAIN
    Nancy 8
MORGAN
    Betsy 103
    Edith   104
    Mary 75
    Molly   103
    Patsy 83
    Polly H. 103

MORGAN
    Sarah 77, 93
MORRIS
    Polly 109
MOSELEY
    Milly 102
MOSS
    Elizabeth 31
    Fanny 69
    Lucy   101
    Martha   95
    Patsy   95
MULLINS
    Elizabeth 67
    Lucy   104
    Mary   38, 104
    Sally   29
    Susannah   59
MUNFORD
    Elizabeth Beverly   77
MURDOCK
    Seller 111
MURFEY
    Nancy 15
MURRAY
    Ann Bolling 21
    Elizabeth   136
    Susanna   108

NAISH
    Jinney 27
    Judith   89
    Nancy   134
NANCE
    Elizabeth 88
    Judith 8
    Molly   8
    Tabitha   84
NANNEY
    Patsy 135
    Tempy   115
NASH
    Lucy 133
    Sarah   35
NEAL
    Anne   53
    Elizabeth   19
    Mary 86
    Nancy   34

NELSON
    Lucy   94
    Nancy Carter   77
NEWTON
    Elizabeth   94
    Milly   132
NICHOLAS
    Ann   55
NICHOLSON
    Mary   15
NOEL
    Elizabeth   88
NOLLEY
    Rebecca   58
NORMENT
    Frances   68
    Janey   43
    Mary   19
    Nancy   114
NORTHINGTON
    Betsy Edwards   90
    Elizabeth   80
    Sarah   29
NOWELL
    Martha   48
NUCKOLS
    Ann   129
NUNNELLY
    Polly   37
NUNNERY
    Sally   123
    Susanna   121

OLIVER
    Elizabeth   25, 78
    Frances   25
ORNSBY
    Elizabeth   45
    Ellender   29
OSLIN
    Elizabeth   15
    Nancy   91
    Polly   113
    Rebecca   136
OVERBY
    Edith   113
    Liddy   86
    Meloda   128
    Nancy D.   16
OVERTON
    Elizabeth   102

OVERTON
    Sally   69
    Susanna   32
    Susannah   127
OWEN
    Susanna   57

PALMER
    Mary   25
    Nancy   136
PAGE
    Betsy   101
    Caty   113
PARHAM
    Ann   78
    Betsy Lelilah   60
    Mary   20
PARKER
    Elizabeth   121
PARRISH
    Mary   123
PARSONS
    Elizabeth   26
PATILLO
    Rebecca   19
PEARCE
    Lucy   117
PEARCY
    Nancy   18
PENNINGTON
    Ann   88, 96
    Anne   93
    Elizabeth   41
    Fatha   78, 92
    Frances   80
    Janney   33
    Lucy   113
    Martha   58
    Mary M.   58
    Polly   131
    Sukey   93
PERSIZE
    Mary   78
PETTUS
    Amey   119
    Elizabeth   110
    Elizabeth Walker   98
    Harriett   76
    Martha   32
    Mary   98
    Sarah   73

PETTUS
Susanna 17, 98
PETTYFORD
Hannah 50
PHILLIPS
Elizabeth 46
Elizabeth H. 31
Jane 97
Mary 72
Nancy 63
Sally E. 97
Susanna 101
PIERCE
Linne 74
PINSON
Elizabeth 10
PITTS
Anne 114
POINDEXTER
Betsy Ann 98
Clarissa 93
Mary 53
Mary S. 98
Nancy Charlotte 52
Patsy 113
Sicily 97
POINTER
Elizabeth 42
POOL
Mary 90
Susanna 88
POOLE
Sarah 9
POWER
Patty 71
POWERS
Rebecca 128
Sally 37
PREWITT
Nancy 15
PUCKETT
Judith 84
Mary 109
Patty 91
Ruth 123
PULLIAM
Mary 9
Sally 133
PULLY
Fanny 88
Rebecca 22
Rebecca J. 52

PURYEAR
Elizabeth 23, 36, 132
Elizabeth P. 87
Franky 11
Jane 39, 47, 68
Lucy 132
Martha 66
Mary 61
Polly 107
Sally Stith 102
Susanna 24

Johannah 102

QUARLES
Polly 98

RAGSDALE
Joannah 59
Rachel 107
Tabitha 87
RAINEY
Dicy 118
Drucilla 71
Fanny 33
Lucinda 100
Martha 36
Mary 48
Nancy 92
READ
Mary 94
READER
Bicy 22
Patsy 73
REAMEY
Anne 31
Patsy 59
REAMY
Anna 59
REAVES
Joanah 124
REDDING
Jinsey 7
RHODES
Fanny 36
RICHARDS
Millicent 122
Rececca 72

RICHARDSON
    Elizabeth 17
RICHESON
    Mary 72
RICKS
    Dolly 129
RIDLEY
    Dolly 85
ROBARDS
    Phebe 104
ROBERTS
    Ann 108
    Biddy 79
    Caty 125
    Elizabeth 106
    Frances 106
    Lucy 105
    Mary 49, 50, 77
    Nancy 60
    Patsy 93
    Rebecca 117
ROBERTSON
    Frances 77
    Mary 108
    Nancy 74
    Sally 107
ROBINSON
    Mary 92
ROFFE
    Elizabeth 20
    Mary C. 21
ROGERS
    Ann B. 75
    Patsy B. 76
ROOK
    Elizabeth 106
    Hannah 13
ROPER
    Polly 58
ROTTENBERRY
    Lucy 36
    Mary 78
    Rainey 54
ROWLETT
    Sally 32
ROYAL
    Mary 9
    Sarah 9
ROYSTER
    Elizabeth 10, 11
    Frances 39

ROYSTER
    Lucy 90
    Rebecca 108
    Rebecca L. 136
    Sarah 20, 102
    Susanna 33
RUDD
    Martha 97
    Nancy 113
    Sally 56, 66
RUFFIN
    Martha 94
RUSSELL
    Elizabeth 73
    Jane Wright 114
    Martha 126
    Mary 38
    Milly 25
    Patsy 37
    Prudence 72
    Sally 73
    Sarah 92
RYLAND
    Jincy J. 25

SALLE'
    Susannah Allgood 110
SALLEY
    Magdala 18
SALLY
    Happy 131
    Mary 121
SAUNDERS
    Elizabeth 126
    Jane 53
    Mary 131
    Milly 135
    Nancy 91
    Ora 40
SAWSBERRY
    Lucy 84
SCOTT
    Minor Parsons 73
    Pheby 28
SEWARD
    Creasy 65
SHORT
    Eddy 123
    Elizabeth 39

SHORT
Elizabeth H. 129
Janey 47
Martha 38
Mary F. 116
Nancy 42
Patsy 16
Polly 67
Rebecca J. 128
Sally 67
SIMMONS
Catherine 43
Lucy 17
Martha 106
SINGLETON
Mary 120
Nancy 42
SKELTON
Patsey 8
SKINNER
Elizabeth 57
SKIPWITH
Helen 32
SMALL
Mary 27
SMITH
Aggy 60
Ann 126
Elizabeth 71, 88, 133
Lucy 52
Martha 43
Mary 49
Mary, Widow 25
Nancy 113, 119
Peggy 14
Polly 130
Pricilla 34
Sarah 7, 124
Susanna 33, 55, 113
Susannah 54
SPAIN
Judy 125
Polly 11
SPARKS
Martha 18
SPEED
Elizabeth 54
Elizabeth I. 118
Lucy 72
Martha 10, 91
Mary 41
Nancy 98
Sarah 22, 41, 58

SPURLOCK
Aggy 82
Milly 124
STAINBACK
Jean 41
Martha Johnson 78
Polly 73
Sarah 92
STANDLEY
Ann 104
Lucy 51
Mary 136
STARLING
Ann 65
STEAGALL
Martha 47
STEGALL
Elizabeth 92
STEMBRIDGE
Polly 105
STEVENS
Polly 27
STEWART
Amy 45
Betsy 127
Celey 87
Dicey 44
Eliza 116
Elizabeth 95
Lina 27
Mahala 112
Mary 31
Milly 127
Nancy 42, 115
Polly 57
Prissey 70
Rebecca 27
Rittah 59
Sally 87
Thurdy 121
STIGALL
Mary 27
STOKES
Mary M. 30
STONE
Catherine 109
Hannah 134
Mary 88
Nancy 25, 69
Polly 76
Sally 128
Susanna 45

STUART
    Lucy 120
    Precilla 117
SUGGETT
    Elizabeth 87
    Lucy 99
    Molly 70
SULLIVANT
    Mary 61
SWEPSON
    Jane 136
    Lucy 115
    Sarah 112
    Susanna 39

TABB
    Elizabeth 13
    Margaret 76
    Mary 52
    Mary, Mrs. 118
TALLEY
    Mary Ann 35
    Patsy 40
TANNER
    Delina 109
    Mary 46
    Mary Ann 15
    Rebecca 100
    Sarah 15
TARRY
    Mary 35
TAYLOR
    Betsy 40
    Elizabeth 132
    Joice Lark 69
    Judith 53
    Lucy 30
    Martha 30, 109
    Mary 19, 65, 110
    Mary C. 22
    Penelope 33, 84
    Polly Jones 130
    Rebeccah 124
    Rebecca B. 100
    Sally 40
    Sarah 38, 77, 118
    Susanna 130
THOMAS
    Elizabeth 107
    Nancy 58, 106

THOMAS
    Nanny 97
THOMASON
    Judith 13
    Polly 112
    Sally 133
    Sukey 27
THOMERSON
    Elizabeth 87
THOMPSON
    Elizabeth 80, 123
    Judith 115
    Letty 45
    Martha 39
    Molly 121
    Nancy 35, 63, 71
    Patsy 13
    Polly 23
    Rebekah 16
    Sarah 108, 121
THORNTON
    Jane 64
    Sally 9
TIBBS
    Sarah 87
TINDAL
    Polly 54
TISDALE
    Becky 111
    Levina 31
    Phebe 121
TOONE
    Martha 73, 96
    Polly 127
    Sarah 29
    Susanna 111
TUCKER
    Amy 36
    Catherine 32, 123
    Elizabeth 36
    Frances 123
    Jane 123
    Lucy 68
    Mary 76
    Mary Thweate 22
    Polly 76
TUDOR
    Milla 97
TURNER
    Betsy 99
    Lucretia 88
    Mary 66, 105

TURNER
    Milly 65
    Nancy 71, 127
    Polly 71
    Sally 70
    Wilmouth 70

UNDERWOOD
    Levinia 130
    Willie 55

VALENTINE
    Lucy 110
VAUGHAN
    Clary 24
    Elizabeth 11, 18
    Elizabeth 113, 134
    Ermer 69
    Fanny 102
    Frances 94
    Hannah 125
    Jane 40
    Martha 66, 70
    Molly 53
    Nancy 28, 89, 128
    Patsy 21, 89
    Polly Mealer 127
    Rebecca 14
    Rody 94
    Sally 67
    Susanna 10
VENABLE
    Anne 83
VOWEL
    Sally 27

WADE
    Isabella 122
    Margaret 60
    Nancy O. 125
    Patsy 60
    Polly 115
    Sarah 67
WAGSTAFF
    Ann Freeman 64
    Elizabeth 40

WAGSTAFF
    Lilly 70
    Mary 42
    Polly 69
    Sally 88
WALDEN
    Mary Hubbard 132
    Polly 117
    Priscilla 116
    Tabitha 22
WALKER
    Agga 49
    Agnes 86
    Ann E. 29
    Elizabeth 35, 44
    Fanny 99
    Jane 46
    Mary 114
    Nancy 109
    Phebe 111
    Polly 45
    Sally 33
    Sally H. 125
    Tabitha 18
WALL
    Caty 29, 43
    Rebecca 62
    Sally 62
WALLER
    Caty 133
    Lucy 61
    Nancy 29
WALTON
    Anne 70
    Barbara 12
WARREN
    Elizabeth 88
    Polly 48
WATKINS
    Mary 120
WATSON
    Charlotte 13
    Frances 79
    Martha 111
    Phebe Malone 135
    Rebecca 39
    Rebeccah 8
    Tabitha 106
WATTS
    Elizabeth H. B. 10
    Frances Anne 121

WEATHERFORD
- Amy 131
- Sarah 114

WEBB
- Leannah Basey 71
- Nancy 30
- Tabitha 59

WEEKES
- Frances 32

WELLS
- Anne 103
- Hannah 86

WESTBROOK
- Phoebe 61

WESTMORELAND
- Mary 51

WHITBY
- Elizabeth Hill 61

WHITE
- Elanner 87
- Elizabeth 40
- Jincy 40
- Mary 13, 46, 59
- Nancy 68

WHITEHEAD
- Elizabeth 30, 119
- Jane 72
- Nancy 50
- Sarah 32

WHITLOW
- Anne 51

WHOBERY
- Molly 57

WHOBERRY
- Nancy 23

WHOBRY
- Sally 16

WILBORN
- Nancy 64

WILBURN
- Elizabeth 126

WILKERSON
- Agnes 136
- Betsy 86

WILES
- Tempe 37

WILLIAMS
- Dorcas 16
- Jane 90
- Martha 53
- Nancy 23
- Obedience 32

WILLIAMS
- Patsy 93
- Sally 67
- Sarah Oslin 41

WILLIAMSON
- Elizabeth 101
- Jincey 12
- Nancy 29

WILLIS
- Mary 55
- Nancy 81

WILLS
- Nancy M. 129

WILSON
- Ann 28
- Elizabeth 29, 101
- Lucy 85
- Mary 58, 114
- Nancy 56
- Susanna 129
- Tabitha 114

WINFIELD
- Dolly 128
- Martha 106
- Mary 106
- Nancy 75

WINKFIELD
- Rebecca 13

WINKLER
- Charlotte 130

WINN
- Elizabeth 85
- Frances 92
- Jane 131
- Nancy 130

WOOTTON
- Elizabeth 39

WORSHAM
- Elizabeth 64, 93
- Polly 10
- Rebecca 11
- Sally 136

WRAY
- Sarah 95

WRIGHT
- Elizabeth 77
- Jane 100
- Martha 124
- Mary 64
- Nancy 39, 48
- Nancy 135, 136
- Polly 42

WRIGHT
        Sally   36
        Sarah L.   31
WYNN
        Kitty   10

YANCEY
        Delphia 122
        Elizabeth   54
        Mary   133
        Nancy   53
        Polly   82

YANCEY
        Susanna 133
        Susannah   96
YATES
        Milly 121
YEARGEN
        Elizabeth 88
        Nancy   89
YOUNG
        Elanor   106
        Judith B.   79
        Lucy   79
        Mary   118
        Susanna   119

ADDENDA

The following Mecklenburg County marriages were found
in the Minister's Returns. Some of the returns do not have complete dates. No bonds were found for these marriages
and they are included as a supplement to the marriage records in this volume.

AKIN, Thomas   Mary Brister
    Minister: Henry Lester   M. May 5, 1785

CIMBEL, Wily *   Nancy Cockrum
    Minister: James Read   M. March 20, 1794
    * Wiley Kimbell ?

COLEY, Thomas   Sally Tucker
    Minister: William Creath   M. March   , 1800

CROWDER, Nathaniel   Nancy Crews
    Minister: William Creath   M. December   , 1799

DAVIS, John   Martha Murray
    Minister: Henry Lester   M. July 30, 1785

DAVIS, William H.   Sarah Allgood
    Minister: James Meacham   M. February 18, 1809

DENTON, Miles   Nancy Stuart
    Minister: William Creath   M. February   , 1802

FAUCET, James   Harriet Farrar
    Minister: James Read   M.   1791

FEATHERSTON, Henry   Nancy Marshall
    Minister: William Richards   M. January 23, 1799

FITTS, John   Cuzza Tabor
    Minister: James Read   M. January 25, 1792

GLASSCOCK, William   Nelly Bowen
    Minister: James Read   M. June 25, 1794

GREGORY, John   Elizabeth Neal
    Minister: John Williams   M. February 7, 1793

GRIFFIN, Elijah   Mary Gold
    Minister: Henry Lester   M. January 20, 1785
    Note: The minister's return has notation Halifax
        County

GRIFFIN, Francis   Susannah Tranum
    Minister: Henry Lester   M. July 23, 1785

HENDRICK, William
    Minister: James Read
    * Rebecca Marrow ?
                        * Beckie Merrah
                        M. June 6, 1794

HOWELL, Allen
    Minister: William Creath
                        Elizabeth Stuart
                        M. July   , 1800

HUDSON, William
    Minister: William Creath
                        Elizabeth Robeson
                        M. September   , 1794

JONES, James B.
    Minister: George Micklejohn
                        Jane J. Davis
                        M. August 3, 1810

KELLEY, James
    Minister: Henry Lester
                        Judy Hardy
                        M. April 24, 1785

MOSS, Thomas
    Minister: Matthew Dance
                        Peggy Barry
                        M. May 7, 1799

OGBURN, Jones
    Minister: William Richards
                        Nancy Fowlkes
                        M. June 15, 1797

OWEN, Thomas
    Minister: James Read
                        Sarah Hamblin
                        M. September   , 1792

POOL, Mitchell
    Minister: William Richards
                        Elizabeth Loafman
                        M. March 13, 1798

ROACH, Simeon
    Minister: John Marshall
                        Jane Allen
                        M. March 18, 1786

ROGERS, George
    Minister: William Richards
                        Polly Stembridge
                        M. November 1, 1810

RUSSELL, Theophilus
    Minister: Charles Ogburn
                        Rhoda Mason
                        M. January 23, 1799

SANDERS, Thomas *
    Minister: John Loyd
    * Thomas Saunders ?
                        Mary Ann Moore
                        M. February 21, 1791

SPEAKS, William Taylor
    Minister: William Creath
                        Maley Gober
                        M. July 19, 1798

STROUD, William
    Minister: James Read
                        Elizabeth Williamson
                        M. May 10, 1793

TANNER, Jonathon
    Minister: John Loyd
                        Sarah Tanner
                        M. December 19, 1793

WILBURN, Killis *
    Minister: James Read
    * Achilles Wilburn - Edith Hardy ?
                        Eade Harde
                  M. September 30, 1793

WILKERSON, William   Lucy Griffin
    Minister: Henry Lester   M. January 21, 1785

WILKINSON, Bentley   Frances Townsend
    Minister: James Read   M. December 28, 1792

WILLS, Eli   Sarah Tuzel
    Minister: William Creath   M. September   , 1795

WORSHAM, Benjamin   Frances Griffin
    Minister: James Read   M. July 8, 1794

WRIGHT, Nathan   Elizabeth Cockerham
    Minister: Henry Lester   M. September 20, 1785

ERRATUM

LAMBERT, Isham   Sally Blanton
    M.B. June 17, 1796   Surety: James Burton

The following marriages have been compiled from the records of adjoining or near by counties.

AKIN, James   Mary Murphy
    M.B. July 9, 1779   Surety: Benjamin McIntosh
    Marriage Record - Caswell County, N. C.

ANDERSON, James   Mary Taylor
    M.B. August 23, 1770   Surety: Joseph Taylor
    Marriage Record - Granville County, N. C.

BAPTIST, William G., Jr.   Elizabeth May
    M.B. January 18, 1806   Minister: Thomas Hardie
    Note: Elizabeth, widow of Stephen May
    Note: William, son of William G. Baptist, Sr.
    Marriage Record - Charlotte County

BASKERVILL, William   Mary Eaton
    M.B. January 22, 1786   Surety: H. E. Johnson
    Note: Mary, daughter of Col. Charles R. Eaton
    Marriage Record - Granville County, N. C.

BILBO, James   Dorothy Clack
    M.B. December 12, 1781   Surety: William Thornton
    Marriage Record - Brunswick County

BILBO, Nicholas   Mary Baskervill
    M.B. September 7, 1784   Surety: George H. Baskervill
    Note: Mary, daughter of George Baskervill, deceased
    Note: Sister of George H. Baskervill
    Marriage Record - Brunswick County

BIRCHETT, Theodrick   Rebecca Collier
    M.B. September 4, 1793   Surety: Isaac Hicks
    Note: Rebecca, daughter of Howell Collier, deceased
    Marriage Record - Brunswick County

BOSWELL, Ranson   Elizabeth Moss
    M.B. November 15, 1790   Surety: B. T. Henderson
    Note: Ranson, son of Ranson Boswell, Sr.
    Marriage Record - Granville County, N. C.

BOTTOM, John   Tabitha Harrison
    M.B. July 17, 1800   Surety: Henry Harrison
    Minister: James Meacham
    Marriage Record - Brunswick County

BOYD, John   Sarah Hester
    M.B. November 15, 1780   Surety: Robert Hester
    Marriage Record - Granville County, N. C.

BOYD, Thomas   Dolly Cox
    M.B. February 8, 1780   Surety: James Yancey
    Marriage Record - Granville County

BOYD, William   Polly Williamson
    M.B. February 13, 1795   Surety: James Williamson
    Marriage Record - Caswell County, N. C.

BRAME, Thomas   Elizabeth Roffe
    M.B. February 11, 1778   Surety: James Brame
    Marriage Record - Granville County, N. C.

BROWN, Shadrach   Mary Nance
    M.B. May 23, 1761
    Marriage Record - Lunenburg County

BUGG, Anderson   Lucy Morgan
    M.B. May 10, 1791   Surety: John Allen
    Marriage Record - Granville County, N. C.

BUGG, John   Sally Malone
    M.B. February 3, 1798   Surety: George Malone
    Minister: William Creath
    Marriage Record - Brunswick County

BUGG, Samuel   Ann Hix
    M.B. June 1, 1757
    Marriage Record - Lunenburg County

BURTON, Allen   Nancy Cleaton
    M.B. January 19, 1791   Surety: Francis Scoggins
    Marriage Record - Caswell County, N. C.

BURTON, Robert   Agatha Williams
    M.B. October 12, 1775   Surety: Thomas Satterwhite
    Note: Agatha, daughter of John and Agnes (Bullock)
          Williams
    Note: Robert, son of Hutchins and Tabitha (Minge)
          Burton
    Marriage Record - Granville County, N. C.

BURTON, Robert   Mary Lewis
    M.B. July 14, 1781   Surety: John Lewis
    Marriage Record - Granville County, N. C.

CAMP, John   Judith Wagstaff
    M.B. August 22, 1766
    Marriage Record - Lunenburg County

CARDIN, James   Elizabeth Fuller
    M.B. January 20, 1784   Surety: Stephen Jones
    Marriage Record - Granville County

CARTER, Theodorick   Sally Eubank
    M.B. November 10, 1763   Surety: Jacob Royster
    Marriage Record - Lunenburg County

CAVENISS, Matthew   Jenny Freeman
    M.B. December 5, 1798   Surety: Anderson Taylor
    Marriage Record - Granville County, N. C.

CHEATHAM, Edward   Nancy Davis
    M.B. February 20, 1792   Surety: Henry Townes
    Marriage Record - Granville County, N. C.

CLAY, John   Hannah Crawley
    M.B. August 26, 1797   Surety: Robert Crawley
    Marriage Record - Granville County, N. C.

COCKE, Peter   Mary Whitehead
    M.B. May 4, 1769   Surety: Richard Whitehead
    Note: Mary, daughter of Richard Whitehead
    Marriage Record - Brunswick County

COLLIER, William   Patty (Martha) Thweatt
    M.B. November 22, 1773   Surety: John Jones
    Note: Patty, daughter of Miles Thweatt, Jr., deceased
    Marriage Record - Brunswick County

COURTNEY, Dr. Clack   Prudence Clarke
    M.B. October 14, 1756   Surety: George Clarke
    Note: Prudence, daughter of George Clarke
    Note: Prudence (Clarke) Courtney married (2) Samuel
          Holmes, Jr. of Mecklenburg County
    Marriage Record - Brunswick County

COX, Bartley   Mary Bouldin
    M.B. November 2, 1768   Surety: Clement Read
    Note: Mary, daughter of Thomas Bouldin
    Marriage Record - Charlotte County

COX, George   Polly Cox
    M.B. December 29, 1799   Surety: Benjamin E. Pinson
    Marriage Record - Granville County, N. C.

COX, Jesse   Elizabeth Farley
    M.B. November 4, 1782   M. November 19, 1782
    Minister: Thomas Johnston   Surety: James Watkins
    Note: Jesse, son of John Cox
    Marriage Record - Charlotte County

COX, John   Francinia Bouldin
    M.B. July 19, 1758   Surety: Thomas Bouldin
    Note: John, Jr., son of John and Mary Cox of
          Mecklenburg County
    Marriage Record - Lunenburg County

COX, William   Sally Stembridge
    Minister: Obadiah Edge   M. November 13, 1785
    Mariage Record - Charlotte County

COX, William   Polly Daniel
    M.B. December 11, 1799   Surety: Sam T. Williams
    Marriage Record - Granville County, N. C.

DANIEL, John   Elizabeth Insco
    M.B. May 1, 1786   Surety: Joseph Daniel
    Marriage Record - Granville County, N. C.

DANIEL, Leonard   Mary Ann Graves
    M.B. December 21, 1789   Surety: Joseph Smith
    Marriage Record - Granville County, N. C.

DANIEL, Martin   Polly Mims
    M.B. February 3, 1795   M. February 6, 1795
    Minister: Edward Almand   Surety: William Vaughan
    Note: Polly, daughter of Mary Mims
    Marriage Record - Charlotte County

DAVIS, William   Elinor Howard
    M.B. March 3, 1756
    Note: Elinor, daughter of Francis and Dianna Howard
    Marriage Record - Lunenburg County

DAVIS, William   Jane Hopkins
    M.B. December 2, 1760
    Marriage Record - Lunenburg County

DAVIS, William   Agnes Lanier
    M.B. August 28, 1769
    Note: Agnes, daughter of William Lanier
    Marriage Record - Brunswick County

DELONY, Henry   Rebecca Walker
    M.B. May 11, 1753   Surety: John Maclin
    Note: Rebecca, widow of Alexander Walker, nee
          Rebecca Broadnax
    Note: Henry Delony of Lunenburg County (Mecklenburg)

EGGLESTON, Thomas   Ann Watson
    M.B. September 10, 1763   Surety: Richard Witton
    Marriage Records - Lunenburg County

ELAM, Joel   Mary Ann Easter
    M.B. February 1, 1790   M. February 3, 1790
    Minister: John Williams   Surety: Hill Hudson
    Marriage Record - Charlotte County

169

FEILD, Hume R   Millane Young
    M.B. December 18, 1797   Surety: Anderson Taylor
    Marriage Record - Granville County, N. C.

FINCH, Claiborn   Sarah Hunt
    M.B. February 26, 1790   Surety: John Finch
    Marriage Record - Granville County, N. C.

GOLD, Pleasant   Sarah Wilson
    M.B. November 19, 1800   Surety: Robert Wilson
    Pleasant Gold, Baptist Minister
    Note: Son of Daniel Gold, deceased, Mecklenburg
          County
    Marriage Record - Granville County, N. C.

GRAVES, David   Nancy Hunt
    M.B. December 19, 1796   Surety: Thomas Hunt
    Marriage Record - Granville County, N. C.

GRAVES, Henry   Nancy Daniel
    M.B. December 2, 1789   Surety: James Smith
    Marriage Record - Granville County, N. C.

GRAVES, John   Penelope Hunt
    M.B. September 17, 1796   Surety: Edmund Hunt
    Marriage Record - Granville County, N. C.

GRAVES, William   Polly Hester
    M.B. December 21, 1798   Surety: James Hester
    Marriage Record - Granville County, N. C.

GRIFFIN, Samuel   Mary Patillo
    M.B. July 7, 1794   Surety: William Norwood
    Marriage Record - Granville County, N. C.

GRIGG, Robert   Susannah Cash
    M.B. December 16, 1781   Surety: Fenton Hall
    Marriage Record - Granville County, N. C.

HARRIS, Claiborn   Sally Hudson
    M.B. December 18, 1789   Surety: Hill Hudson
    Note: Sally, daughter of Daniel Hudson
    Marriage Record - Charlotte County

HAWKINS, Thomas   Mary Howard
    M.B. January 29, 1753
    Marriage Record - Lunenburg County

HESTER, Benjamin   Molly Dyer
    M.B. December 23, 1778   Surety: Reuben Talley
    Marriage Record - Granville County, N. C.

HESTER, Francis   Elizabeth Blanks
    M.B. September 29, 1795   Surety: Francis Royster
    Marriage Record - Granville County, N. C.

HESTER, Henry   Mary Graves
    M.B. November 8, 1774   Surety: Robert Hester
    Marriage Record - Granville County, N. C.

HESTER, John   Mary Whitfield
    M.B. December 29, 1796
    Marriage Record - Granville County, N. C.

HESTER, Joseph   Elizabeth Parker
    M.B. July 4, 1781   Surety: Barnett Gilliam
    Marriage Record - Granville County, N. C.

HESTER, Robert   Lily Daniel
    M.B. April 29, 1785
    Marriage Record - Granville County, N. C.

HESTER, Robert   Barbara Smith
    M.B. November 5, 1788   Surety: James Smith
    Marriage Record - Granville County, N. C.

HESTER, Stephen   Elizabeth Smith
    M.B. December 19, 1791   Surety: Thomas Daniel
    Marriage Record - Granville County, N. C.

HESTER, Thomas   Elizabeth Stovall
    M.B. May 8, 1798   Surety: Francis Royster
    Marriage Record - Granville County, N. C.

HESTER, William   Mary Frazier
    M.B. December 27, 1780   Surety: Frederick Rives
    Marriage Record - Granville County, N. C.

HINTON, David   Jane Lewis
    M.B. November 13, 1790   Surety: Thomas Hines
    Marriage Record - Granville County, N. C.

HIX, William   Elizabeth Ann Tatum
    M.B. March 14, 1778   Surety: John Potter
    Marriage Record - Granville County, N. C.

HOLMES, Edward   Hannah Matthews
    M.B. March 5, 1791   Surety: William Mitchell
    Minister: John Fore
    Note: Edward Holmes of Mecklenburg County
    Marriage Record - Brunswick County

HOLMES, Isaac   Frances Parham
    M.B. December 13, 1797   Surety: John C. Courtney
    Marriage Record - Brunswick County

HOLMES, William   Sarah Warren
    M.B. June 15, 1782   Surety: * Sack Pennington
    * Isaac Pennington
    Note: Sarah, widow of John Warren
    Marriage Record - Brunswick County

HOPKINS, Arthur   Judith Jefferson
    M.B. September 7, 1762
    Marriage Record - Lunenburg County

HOWARD, George   Catherine Graves
    M.B. February 12, 1792   Surety: Thomas Owen
    Marriage Record - Granville County, N. C.

HOWARD, Henry   Priscilla Farrar
    M.B. May 4, 1762
    Marriage Record - Lunenburg County

HUNT, John   Frances Penn
    M.B. August 5, 1771   Surety: James Hunt
    Marriage Record - Granville County, N. C.

HUNT, Samuel   Sarah Howard
    M.B. May 20, 1780   Surety: James Hunt
    Marriage Record - Granville County, N. C.

HYDE, Robert   Elizabeth Harper
    M.B. October 22, 1781   Surety: Thomas Lanier
    Marriage Record - Granville County, N. C.

JEFFERSON, Feild   Mary Allen
    M.B. October 31, 1753   (Widow)
    Marriage Record - Lunenburg County

JONES, Richard, Jr.   Lucy Clay
    M.B. June 26, 1771   Surety: * Richard Whitton, Jr.
    * Richard Witton, Jr.
    Note: Lucy, ward of Marston Clay
    Note: Richard, son of Richard Jones, Sr.
    Marriage Record - Charlotte County

KENNON, Charles   Mary Lewis
    M.B. April 19, 1770   Surety: Joseph Taylor
    Marriage Record - Granville County, N. C.

KENNON, William   Betsy Bullock
    M.B. March 11, 1771   Surety: William Bullock
    Marriage Record - Granville County, N. C.

KING, Myles   Elizabeth Potter
    M.B. September 11, 1779   Surety: Arthur Jordan
    Marriage Record - Granville County, N. C.

LANIER, Lewis   Martha Speed
    M.B. November 25, 1752   Surety: James Speed
    Marriage Record - Brunswick County

LEWIS, Nathaniel   Sally Harris
    M.B. November 29, 1790   Surety: Thomas Owen
    Marriage Record - Granville County, N. C.

LEWIS, William   Elizabeth Howard
    M.B. October 21, 1773   Surety: Graves Howard
    Marriage Record - Granville County, N. C.

LEWIS, Willis   Mary Ann Taylor
    M.B. October 10, 1790   Surety: Charles Lewis
    Marriage Record - Granville County, N. C.

LUCAS, John   Elizabeth Comer
    M.B. October 27, 1762
    Marriage Record - Lunenburg County

McADEN, Hugh   Catherine Scott
    M.B. October 11, 1762
    Note: Hugh McAden died in Milton, N. C.
    Note: Hugh McAden father of Rev. James McAden of
            Mecklenburg County
    Marriage Record - Lunenburg County

MACLIN, James M.   Rebecca Cunningham
    M. May 11, 1753
    Charlotte County - Marriage Record

McQUAY, John *   Sally M. Goode
    M.B. November 21, 1788   Surety: Langston Bacon
    * John McQuie
    Note: Sally, daughter of Mackness Goode
    Marriage Record - Charlotte County

MABRY, Jordan   Ann Harwell
    M.B. September 10, 1770   Surety: John Clack
    Consent: Joshua Mabry, father of Jordan
    Consent: James Harwell, father of Ann
    Note: Jordan Mabry of Mecklenburg County
    Marriage Record - Brunswick County

McCRAW, Dancy   Elizabeth Pugh
    M.B. December 31, 1797   Surety: John Pugh
    Note: Elizabeth, daughter of Samuel Pugh
    Note: Dancy, son of Stephen McCraw
    Marriage Record - Charlotte County

MARABLE, William   * Judith More
     M.B. October 3, 1760   * Judith Moore
     Marriage Record - Charlotte County

MARSHALL, Alexander   Anne Walthall
     M.B. July 17, 1787   Minister: John Cameron
     Marriage Record - Chesterfield County

MARSHALL, James   Mary Williams
     M.B. January 5, 1789   Surety: Lewis Williams
     Marriage Record - Brunswick County

MAYES, Frederick   Martha Hinton
                              Surety: James Atkins
     M.B. October 3, 1792
     Marriage Record - Granville County, N. C.

MINOR, Joseph   Edith Cox
     M.B. October 11, 1750
     Note: Edith, daughter of John and Mary Cox of
          Mecklenburg County.
     Marriage Record - Lunenburg County

MITCHELL, Daniel   Mary Grigg
     M.B. November 26, 1763   Surety: William Grigg
     Marriage Record - Granville County, N. C.

NELSON, Major John   Nancy (Anne) Carter
     M. July 25, 1781
     Note: Major John Nelson of "Oak Hill" Mecklenburg
          County - Married in the Chapel at William and
          Mary College

OVERBY, Peter   Indiana Stovall
     M.B. July 1, 1797   Surety: Phillip Yancey
     Marriage Record - Granville County, N. C.

PALMER, William   Mary Bressie
     M.B. May 25, 1776   Surety: James Yancey
     Marriage Record - Granville County, N. C.

PARHAM, Kennon   Milly Parham
     M.B. July 28, 1783   Surety: Lewis Parham
     Marriage Record - Granville County, N. C.

PATILLO, Anderson   Catherine Harper
     M.B. Oct. 20, 1792   Surety: Robert Hyde
     Marriage Record - Granville County, N. C.

PEASLEY, William   Lucy Saunders
     M.B. November 8, 1764   Surety: Richard Swepson
     Marriage Record - Lunenburg County

PENNINGTON, William   Drusilla Smithson
    M.B. November 25, 1780
    Marriage Record - Lunenburg County

PINSON, James   Sarah Dupree
    M.B. March 24, 1792   Surety: Joseph Glenn
    Consent: Lewis Dupree, father of Sarah
    Marriage Record - Halifax County, Va.

POINDEXTER, Francis   Jane Lanier
    M.B. May 26, 1786   Surety: Henry Patillo
    Marriage Record - Granville County, N. C.

POINDEXTER, Philip   Sarah Crymes
    M.B. August 15, 1761
    Marriage Record - Lunenburg County

POTTER, William   Elizabeth Potter
    M.B. November 9; 1773   Surety; Abraham Potter
    Marriage Record - Granville County, N. C.

RIDLEY, James   Elizabeth Lewis
    M.B. October 14, 1801   Surety: Hutchins G. Burton
    Marriage Record - Granville County, N. C.

ROBERTSON, John   Molly Weatherford
    M.B. July 27, 1781
    Marriage Record - Lunenburg County

ROYSTER, David   Mary Daniel
    M.B. January 11, 1775   Surety: Thomas Henderson
    Note: David, son of Jacob and Patty Royster of
          Mecklenburg County
    Note: Mary, daughter of James and Sarah Daniel of
          Granville County, N. C.
    Marriage Record - Granville County, N. C.

ROYSTER, Francis   Elizabeth Shepard
    M.B. May 6, 1789   Surety: J. Redford
    Marriage Record - Granville County, N. C.

ROYSTER, John   * Phiby Stovall
    M.B. August 6, 1792   Surety: Thomas Apling
    * Phebe Stovall
    Marriage Record - Granville County, N. C.

ROYSTER, William   Sarah Puryear
    M.B. June 28, 1779   Surety: William Puryear
    Marriage Record - Granville County, N. C.

RUSSELL, Richard   Elizabeth Carlton
    M.B. July 7, 1761
    Note: Elizabeth Carlton married (2) Moses Overton of
          Mecklenburg County
    Marriage Record - Lunenburg County

SAUNDERS, Edward   Jane Yancey
    M.B. December 22, 1774   Surety: Jesse Saunders
    Note: Jane, daughter of James Yancey of Granville
          County, N. C.
    Note: Edward Saunders of Mecklenburg County, brother
          of Jesse Saunders
    Marriage Record - Granville County, N. C.

SAUNDERS, Jesse   Annis Yancey
    M.B. October 19, 1765   Surety: James Yancey
    Note: Jesse Saunders of Mecklenburg County
    Note: Annis Yancey, daughter of James Yancey of
          Granville County
    Marriage Record - Granville County, N. C.

SAUNDERS, John   Mary Paris
    M.B. November 1, 1765   Surety: Jacob Slaughter
    Note: John Saunders of Mecklenburg County
    Marriage Record - Granville County, N. C.

SKIPWITH, Peyton   Jane (Jean) Miller
    M.B. September 25, 1788   Surety: Robert Burton
    Note: A memorandum with the Skipwith Papers in the
          Archives of the Library of the College of
          William and Mary states that Sir Peyton
          Skipwith and Jean Miller were married in 1788
    Note: Sir Peyton Skipwith of "Prestwould",
          Mecklenburg County
    Marriage Record - Granville County, N. C.

SMITH, Anderson   Sally Hunt
    M.B. October 15, 1782   Surety: Bennett Searcy
    Note: Anderson, son of Drury Smith of Mecklenburg
          County
    Note: Sally, daughter of William Hunt of Granville
          County, N. C.
    Marriage Record - Granville County, N. C.

SPEED, Joseph   Mary G. Harper
    M.B. December 22, 1796   Surety: William Shepard
    Marriage Record - Granville County, N. C.

STAINBACK, John   Patty Davis
    M.B. July 7, 1769   Surety: William Wilson
    Marriage Record - Granville County, N. C.

STANDLEY, William   Lucy Prewitt
    M.B. December 15, 1766   Surety: Bartholomew Stovall
    Marriage Record - Granville County, N. C.

STROUD, George   Rachel Insco
    M.B. August 23, 1799   Surety: William Insco
    Marriage Record - Granville County, N. C.

SUGGETT, Edgecomb   Molly Jones
    M.B. July 23, 1789   Surety: John Jones
    Note: Molly, daughter of Stephen Jones
    Note: Edgecomb Suggett of Mecklenburg County
    Note: Edgecomb Suggett married (1) Constance Edmund-
        son of Amelia County
    Marriage Record - Brunswick County

TAYLOR, Anderson   Jane Young
    M.B. December 20, 1790   Surety: John Young
    Marriage Record - Granville County, N. C.

TAYLOR, Edmund   Patsy Lewis
    M.B. April 24, 1790   Surety: Henry Potter
    Note: Edmund (Jr.), son of Edmund Taylor

TAYLOR, Edmond   Polly Robards
    M.B. September 10, 1798   Surety: Joseph White
    Note: Edmond and Edmund Taylor may have been same
    Both marriage records in Granville County, N. C.

TAYLOR, James   Sally Eaton
    M.B. March 16, 1784   Surety: Bennett Eaton
    Note: James, son of Edmund Taylor
    Marriage Record - Granville County, N. C.

TAYLOR, James   Betsy Robards
    M.B. October 15, 1797   Surety: Edmund Taylor
    Marriage Record - Granville County, N. C.

TAYLOR, John   Susannah Bullock
    M.B. March 16, 1784   Surety: Edmund Taylor
    Note: John, son of Edmund Taylor
    Marriage Record - Granville County, N. C.

THOMASON, William   * Mary Reaves
    M.B. November 23, 1782   Surety: William Thomason
    * Mary Rives
    Marriage Record - Granville County, N. C.

WADE, Benjamin   Amy Jordan
    M.B. May 11, 1762   Surety: Phillip Taylor
    Note: Phillip Taylor, son of John Taylor and brother
        of Edmund Taylor, Sr.
    Marriage Record - Granville County, N. C.

WADE, Robert   Rebecca Downy
     M.B. August 8, 1775   Surety: Robert Downy
     Marriage Record - Granville County, N. C.

WALKER, Daniel   Nancy Bailey
     M.B. June 27, 1798   Surety: William Walker
     Marriage Record - Granville County, N. C.

WEATHERFORD, Major   Mary Edwards
     M.B. May 26, 1760
     Marriage Record - Lunenburg County

WHITEHEAD, Benjamin   Elizabeth Swepson
     M.B. March 31, 1761
     Marriage Record - Lunenburg County

WOOTEN, John *   Polly Johnson
     M.B. July 26, 1796   Surety: Joseph Johnson
     * John Wootton
     Marriage Record - Granville County, N. C.

WORSHAM, Joshua   Ann Hopkins
     M.B. January 15, 1794   Surety: George Hopkins
     Marriage Record - Granville County, N. C.

WORTHAM, James   Sarah Lewis
     M.B. September 20, 1789   Surety: William Marshall
     Marriage Record - Granville County, N. C.

WRIGHT, William   Mary Hester
     M.B. June 9, 1797   Surety: William Hester
     Marriage Record - Granville County, N. C.

YANCEY, Absolom   Henrietta Nuckols
     M.B. January 26, 1789   Surety: James Nuckols
     Note: Absolom Yancey of Mecklenburg County
     Marriage Record - Louisa County

YANCEY, James   Mary Bracey
     M.B. August 15, 1765   Surety: William Wood
     Marriage Record - Granville County, N. C.

YANCEY, Richard   Mary Walton
     M.B. December 30, 1796
     Consent: Mary Yancey, mother of Mary
     Note: Richard Yancey of Mecklenburg County
     Marriage Record - Louisa County

YANCEY, William   Abigail Hicks
     M.B. November 13, 1767   Surety: James Yancey
     Marriage Record - Granville County, N. C.

I N D E X

FARRAR
    Harriet 163
    Priscilla 172
FOWLKES
    Nancy 164
FRAZIER
    Mary 171
FREEMAN
    Jenny 168
FULLER
    Elizabeth 167

GOBER
    Maley 164
GOLD
    Mary 163
GOODE
    Sally M. 173
GRAVES
    Catherine 172
    Mary 171
    Mary Ann 169
GRIFFIN
    Frances 165
    Lucy 165
GRIGG
    Mary 174

HAMBLIN
    Sarah 164
HARDE
    Eade 164
HARDY
    Judy 164
HARPER
    Catherine 174
    Elizabeth 172
    Mary G. 176
HARRIS
    Sally 173
HARRISON
    Tabitha 166
HARWELL
    Ann 173
HESTER
    Mary 178
    Polly 170
    Sarah 166
HICKS
    Abigail 178

HINTON
    Martha 174
HIX
    Ann 167
HOPKINS
    Ann 178
    Jane 169
HOWARD
    Elinor 169
    Elizabeth 173
    Mary 170
    Sarah 172
HUDSON
    Sally 170
HUNT
    Nancy 170
    Penelope 170
    Sally 176
    Sarah 170

INSCO
    Elizabeth 169
    Rachel 177

JEFFERSON
    Judith 172
JOHNSON
    Polly 178
JONES
    Molly 177
JORDAN
    Amy 177

LANIER
    Agnes 169
    Jane 175
LEWIS
    Elizabeth 175
    Jane 171
    Mary 172, 167
    Patsy 177
    Sarah 178
LOAFMAN
    Elizabeth 164

MALONE
    Sally 167

MARSHALL
   Nancy 163
MASON
   Rhoda   164
MATTHEWS
   Hannah 171
MAY
   Elizabeth (Widow) 166
MERRAH
   Beckie   164
MILLER
   Jane (Jean) 176
MIMS
   Polly   169
MORE
   Judith   174
MOORE
   Mary Ann   164
MORGAN
   Lucy   167
MOSS
   Elizabeth 166
MURPHY
   Mary   166
MURRAY
   Martha   163

NANCE
   Mary 167
NEAL
   Elizabeth 163
NUCKOLS
   Henrietta 178

PARHAM
   Frances 171
   Milly   174
PARIS
   Mary 176
PARKER
   Elizabeth 171
PATILLO
   Mary 170
PENN
   Frances 172
POTTER
   Elizabeth 175, 172
PREWITT
   Lucy   177

PUGH
   Elizabeth 173
PURYEAR
   Sarah   175

REAVES
   Mary   177
ROBARDS
   Betsy 177
   Polly   177
ROBESON
   Elizabeth 164
ROFFE
   Elizabeth 167

SAUNDERS
   Lucy   174
SCOTT
   Catherine 173
SHEPARD
   Elizabeth   175
SMITH
   Barbara   171
   Elizabeth   171
SMITHSON
   Drusilla 175
SPEED
   Martha   173
STEMBRIDGE
   Polly   164
   Sally   169
STOVALL
   Elizabeth 171
   Indiana   174
   Phiby   175
STUART
   Elizabeth   164
   Nancy   163
SWEPSON
   Elizabeth   178

TABOR
   Cuzza   163
TANNER
   Sarah 164
TATUM
   Elizabeth Ann 171

MINISTERS

ALMAND, Edward
ATKINSON, John

BRAME, Samuel D.
BROWN, Aaron

COX, Phillip
CREATH, William

DABBS, Richard
DANCE, Matthew
DROMGOOLE, Edward

EASTER, John
   "   , Matthew L.
EZELL, Baalam

HAGGARD, Rice
HARDIE, Thomas
HATCHELL, William
HAY, Alexander
HEATH, William

JARROTT, Devereaux

KING, John

LESTER, Henry
LOYD, John

McCARGO, David

MACGOWAN, Ebenezer
MARSHALL, John
MEACHAM, James
MICKLEJOHN, George

NEBLETT, John

OGBURN, Charles
   "   , Henry

PATILLO, Henry
PHAUP, John

READ, James
RICHARDS, William
ROBERTSON, Milton

SCOTT, Thomas
SHELBURNE, James
STEWART, S. S.

TOLLESON, James

WATKINS, James
WILLIAMS, John

The denominational affiliation of most of the ministers listed is unknown, and the minister's returns do not
show, with one exception, the place of residence.

The returns of Alexander Hay give his address as Antrim Glebe, Antrim Parish, Halifax County.

We know, however, from other records that Henry Lester, John Marshall and James Read were Baptist; and that
Aaron Brown, William Heath and Charles Ogburn were Method-
ist.

Edward Almand, Richard Dabbs, Matthew Dance and James
Shelburne were ministers in Lunenburg County.

David McCargo was a minister in Charlotte County; and
Milton Robertson was a minister in Granville County, N. C.

NOTES ON MARRIAGE RECORDS

In compiling this volume of early marriage records of Mecklenburg County, it was deemed advisable to examine the marriage records of Granville County, North Carolina, because of the close association of the early families in the two counties.

Many of the early residents of Granville County had settled first in Mecklenburg and later moved to Granville. Colonial Granville County was established in the same year, 1746, in which Lunenburg County was created. Warren, Vance and the present Granville, all bordering on Mecklenburg County, were a part of Colonial Granville County. Many of the early Mecklenburg County people owned land on both sides of the state line dividing the two counties; and in many of the early wills reference is made to land owned in North Carolina.

Until well into this century, the Roanoke River proved to be a social, as well as economic, barrier since to visit or transact business north of the river meant considerable travel to the nearest ferry. This was particularly true for those residing along the boundary line. As a result, the area of Mecklenburg County lying south of the Roanoke River was more closely allied, both socially and economically, with Granville County than with the area north of the river.

It is necessary, therefore, for one tracing family lineages to know the section of Mecklenburg County in which the family or person resided. Because of the division and settlement of early estates, one member of a family might be found owning land in Mecklenburg while another owned land in Granville County. The member residing in Mecklenburg County, in many cases, will be found to have married in Granville County; and just as frequently a member of the family living in Granville County was married in Mecklenburg County.

Since the deeds, wills, marriage and other records of the area comprising Mecklenburg County were recorded in Lunenburg County from 1746 to 1765, it seemed desirable to examine the records of Lunenburg County also. It is unfortunate that many of the early records of Lunenburg County have not survived the ravages and vicissitudes of time; and that there are few marriage records before 1780 that have been preserved.

The recorded records in other counties adjoining Mecklenburg have been checked but there are few that can

be identified as pertaining to Mecklenburg County. In this
volume, there is listed 145 marriage records from other
counties. All of them bear names to be found in early records of Mecklenburg County. Some are easily identified
as being from Mecklenburg County. It was infeasible to
examine or trace these records in detail, and some of the
records will undoubtedly be found not applicable to Mecklenburg County. The primary purpose, in presenting this
short list, has been to place before the researcher some
other sources of marriage records pertaining to Mecklenburg County.

Notes have been added under many of the marriage records in this volume. These notes have been taken from abstracts of wills, and from other records collected and
owned by the compilers.

The abbreviations used in this volume follow the format used in the volume "Marriage Records - 1811-1853" published in 1962. The date of the marriage bond is listed
on the left under the name of the groom. The actual date
of marriage, if found or different from the date of the
bond, is listed on the right under the name of the bride.

Variations in spelling of Mecklenburg County names
are listed below. Other notes have been added which the
compiler believes will be of interest to the researcher
and to the historian.

<u>MECKLENBURG COUNTY</u>

Robert Munford, Richard Witton, John Speed, Henry Delony,
Edmund Taylor, Benjamin Baird, John Camp, Thomas Erskine,
John Potter, John Cox, Thomas Anderson, John Speed, Jr.
and Samuel Hopkins, Gentlemen, acting under a Commission,
dated March 1, 1765, from Francis Fauquier, Esquire, Lt.
Gov. of the Colony and Dominion of Virginia, met at the
home of Richard Swepson on Monday, March 11, 1765, and
there organized the first county government for the new
county of Mecklenburg.

The first Court for Mecklenburg County was held in the
home of Richard Swepson on Monday, March 11, 1765.

<u>PRESENT</u>

Robert Munford	Thomas Anderson)	
John Camp	John Cox)	Gentleman
Thomas Erskine	John Speed, Junr.)	Justices
John Potter	Samuel Hopkins)	

VARIATIONS IN NAMES

There are variations in spelling of many of the names of Mecklenburg County families. These variations are to be noticed particurlarly in the marriage bonds and on the returns of ministers. At times, the name filled in on the bond, the signature on the bond and name on the minister's return will each be different. Some of these variations are listed here:

Atkins, Adkins; Avary, Avery, Avory; Baskervill, Baskerville; Benford, Binford; Bressie, Bracey; Burrows, Burrus; Chavous, Chavis; Claiborne, Cliborne; Connaway, Conway; Cousins, Couzens; Daly, Daley, Dailey; Dupree, Duprey; Edmondson, Edmundson; Apperson, Epperson; Fargeson, Ferguson; Frasar, Fraser, Frazer, Frazier; Hailey, Haley; Hamblin, Hamlin; Hethcock, Heathcock; Hudson, Hutson; Jeffries, Jeffress; Kelley, Kelly; Maclin, McLin, Macklin; MacGowan, Macgowan; Morgan, Morgain; Murfey, Murphy; Nash, Naish; Norment, Norman; Nowel, Nowell, Noel; Nunnelly, Nunnery; Pool, Poole; Reamy, Reamey; Roffe, Rolfe; Stegall, Steagall, Stigall; Thomason, Thomerson; Winfield, Wingfield, Winkfield; Winn, Wynn.

The spelling of the names used in this volume is that found on the marriage bonds.

OTHER NOTES

BURTON, Robert

"ROBERT BURTON was a delegate from North Carolina; born in MECKLENBURG COUNTY, VIRGINIA, October 20, 1747; moved to Granville County, North Carolina, in 1775; served in Revolutionary Army, and attained the rank of COLONEL; sat in the CONTINENTAL CONGRESS in 1787-1788; member of the commission which established the boundary line between North Carolina, South Carolina and Georgia in 1801; died in Granville County, North Carolina, on May 31, 1825".

CONGRESSIONAL DIRECTORY - 1774-1911

NELSON, Major John

John Nelson, brother of Governor Thomas Nelson, and son of Secretary Nelson of York, was appointed a Captain in the First Regiment of Cavalry in 1776 under Colonel Bland. He was later appointed a Major of the Virginia State Cavalry and served until 14 February 1782.

Johh Nelson married Nancy (Anne) Carter July 25, 1781 in the Chapel at William and Mary College. He died at

"Oak Hill", his home in Mecklenburg County, on February 18, 1827.

15, November, 1837 - Nancy Nelson, age 74, of Mecklenburg County, Virginia, applied for a pension as the widow of Major John Nelson.
Notes from Pension Application of Nancy (Carter) Nelson

DELONY, Henry

Henry Delony, Justice and a Member of the Committee of Safety for Mecklenburg County during the Revolutionary War, married (1), it appears, a daughter of Feild Jefferson. In his will dated June 8, 1762, Feild Jefferson mentions his granddaughter Mary Delony. He appointed Henry Delony and sons Peter Feild, George and John Jefferson as his executors.

Henry Delony married (2) Rebecca Broadnax Walker, widow of Alexander Walker, deceased, of Brunswick County. Rebecca Broadnax Walker had one child by her first marriage - a son Edward Broadnax Walker.

Henry Delony was a son of Lewis Delony who was a Justice of Lunenburg County when it was created in 1746. Henry Delony died sometime after April 29, 1785, but before June 13, 1785 at his home, "Sycamore Lodge", in Mecklenburg County.

ANDERSON, Thomas

Thomas Anderson came to Mecklenburg County as an overseer for Col. William Byrd. He is listed in the tithe list for 1764 as owner of 1050 acres of land. Though no records have been found, he was without doubt married twice, and wife Sarah, named in will, was his (2) wife. He named both married and minor children. His children intermarried with the Taylor, Jones and Lewis families of Mecklenburg and neighboring Granville County, N. C.

ROYSTER FAMILY

Jacob and William Royster came to Mecklenburg County as overseers for Col. William Byrd also. They were the progenitors of the Roysters of Mecklenburg and Granville County, N. C.

TARRY, Samuel

Samuel Tarry of Amelia County - a native of England - left a will dated in Amelia County, June 10, 1757, which was probated in Mecklenburg County June 10, 1765. He was the ancestor of the Tarry family of Mecklenburg County.

BASKERVILL, George

George Baskervill, the immediate progenitor of this Mecklenburg County family, was married twice. The children of the (1) marriage were: John Baskervill and Ann (Baskervill) Lucas, wife of William Lucas. The children of the (2) marriage were: William Baskervill, Martha Baskervill, Mary Baskervill and George Hunt Baskervill. The names of his wives are not known.

George Baskervill was a member of the first Committee of Safety for Mecklenburg County. He died before November 10, 1777 when his will, dated November 17, 1768 was probated in Mecklenburg County.

TAYLOR, Edmund

Edmund Taylor, who married Anne Lewis, was associated with the government of Mecklenburg County from its creation when he was appointed first Surveyor of the county.

He served as a Justice for many years; and was a member of the Committee of Safety. He was a Vestryman of St. James Parish. He subsequently removed to Granville County, N. C., where he died in 1808.

JEFFERSON, Feild

Feild Jefferson, son of Thomas Jefferson, II, of Henrice County, was an early settler in the area that later became Mecklenburg County. Feild Jefferson was an uncle of President Thomas Jefferson.

One of the first deeds recorded in Lunenburg County, after its formation, was a deed from William Howard to Feild Jefferson.

Feild Jefferson had acquired land on the Roanoke River by patent much earlier; and one of the first ferries over the Roanoke River was from his land on the north side of the river to his land on the south side.

The will of Feild Jefferson was probated June 10, 1765, and is recorded on page 4 of Will Book 1, Mecklenburg County.

BURWELL, Thacker

Thacker Burwell, son of Nathaniel Burwell, was a Justice, a member of the Committee of Safety and served as a Lieutenant Colonel in the Second Battalion of Mecklenburg County Militia.

Thacker Burwell died in Mecklenburg County in 1780, and his will was probated on December 11, 1780.

BURWELL, Lewis of "Stoneland"

Lewis Burwell, son of Armistead Burwell, was married twice. He married (1) Ann Spotswood, and (2) Elizabeth Harrison. He was a Justice for many years, and a member of the Committee of Safety for Mecklenburg County during the Revolutionary War. He was in command, as Colonel, of the First Battalion of Mecklenburg Militia. Colonel Burwell was the largest land owner in Mecklenburg County. He is listed in the tithe list for 1764 as owner of three plantations totaling 10,866 acres of land. His will was recorded in Mecklenburg County September 8, 1800.

MUNFORD, Robert of "Richland"

Robert Munford, son of Robert and Anna (Bland) Munford, married Anna Beverly, daughter of William Beverly of "Blandfield", Essex County. Robert Munford was identified with government of Mecklenburg County from its formation on the 11th of March, 1765, until his death. He served for many years as a Justice; he was a member of the second Committee of Safety; and served as County Lieutenant from 1765 until his death in 1784.

SKIPWITH, Sir Peyton of "Prestwould"

Sir Peyton Skipwith, son of Sir William Skipwith of Prince George County, married (1) Anne Miller, daughter of Hugh Miller. Sir Peyton lived first at "Elm Hill" in Mecklenburg County, but after completing "Prestwould" on his Bluestone Plantation moved there to live. He was a Justice for Mecklenburg County; a member of the Committee of Safety, and served as Sheriff of the county in 1777.

During the Revolutionary War, Sir Peyton leased Hog Island and the adjacent mainland plantation and moved there to live. While he lived there, livestock was kept at Hog Island to provision the French Forces aiding America in the war.

Sir Peyton's first wife, Anne Skipwith, died while they lived at Hog Island. Sir Peyton married (2) Jane (Jean) Miller, younger sister of his first wife, in 1788. The marriage bond, with Robert Burton as surety, is in Granville County, N. C.

TABB, John

John Tabb, the first Clerk of Mecklenburg County, was a descendant of the Tabb's of eastern Virginia. He died in 1775. His wife, Mary Tabb, married (2) Richard Swepson, who qualified as guardian for the minor children of John Tabb.

MILITIA OFFICERS

The first Militia Officers for Mecklenburg County who were commissioned by Lt. Gov. Francis Fauquier and took the oath of office before the first court were:

County Lieutenant: Robert Munford

Colonels: Edmund Taylor - Robert Alexander

Major: Benjamin Baird

Quartermaster: John Tabb

Captains: Jacob Royster - Tignal Jones, Senr.-
                    John Potter - Samuel Bugg - Dennis
                    Lark

THE FIRST VESTRY FOR St. JAMES PARISH - June 1761

John Potter	Thomas Moon	)
Joseph Truman	John Camp	) Vestrymen
John Speed	William Hunt	)
Thomas Lanier	Richard Swepson	)

HESTER FAMILY

The Hesters of Mecklenburg County, Va., and Granville County, N. C., were descendants of Francis Hester of New Kent County. They came to Mecklenburg and Granvill from Louisa County.

COX, John

John Cox, named in the Commission for organizing the County, was the son of John and Mary Cox who were early settlers in Lunenburg County. John Cox lived in the Finney Wood section in the northwest corner of the county. He married Francinia Bouldin, daughter of Thomas Bouldin, of Charlotte County

LARGE LAND OWNERS - 1764 - 1000 or MORE ACRES

Thomas Anderson	Drury Malone	Theophilus Feild
John Armistead, Jr.	Robert Munford	Feild Jefferson
Hutchins Burton	Robert Ruffim	Henry Delony
Howell Collier	Edmund Taylor	Stephen Evans, Sr.
Capt. Wm. Davis	Thomas Taylor	Edward Goode
Col. Wm. Harwood	Samuel Young	Branch Tanner
Henry Howard	Samuel Tarry	Benj. Whitehead
Peter Jones	Henry Wilson	John Robertson
Robert Jones	Lewis Burwell	Armistead Burwell
James Lewis	Joseph Boswell	Jacob Michaux, Jr.

MARRIAGE RECORDS 1765 - 1810 MECKLENBURG
COUNTY, VIRGINIA

Addenda and Errata

P. 7 - Abernathy, Signal not Tignal.

P. 9 - Allgood, Jeremiah - Jincy, not Jinney, Claunch.

P. 10 - Apperson, Samuel - 15 Oct. 1801 - Polly Worsham.
    Consent: John Worsham, Senr. father.

P. 10 - Ashton, Henry
    Consent: Richard Watts.

P. 13 - Barner, not Barnes, John.

P. 13 - Banes, not Barnes, Phillip.

P. 14 - Baugh, Daniel - Lucy Brooks, spinster.
    M.B. October 18, not 10, 1780.

P. 14 - Baugh, William B.
    Note: William Baugh, not Batte, son of James Baugh, deceased.

P. 15 - Bilbo, Allen Moss
    Consent: John Farrar, father of Martha Farrar.

P. 16 - Binford, Thomas   Susanna Tinch, not Finch
    M.B. May 7, 1795   Surety: William Tinch

P. 17 - Boswell, Joseph
    Surety: William, not Samuel, Pettus, Senr.
    Delete - Note: Joseph, son of Ransom and Martha Boswell.

P. 18 - Bowen, Hughbe, not Hughke.

P. 18 - Boyd, Robert
    Note: Tabitha Walker, daughter of Henry and Martha Bolling
        Eppes Walker.

P. 19 - Boynton, Elijah S.

P. 20 - Brandon or Brandum, Edward.

P. 22 - Bugg, William
    M.B. October, not November 7, 1773.

P. 23 - Burrus, Willie, not Wiley.

P. 23 - Burton, Allen   Rebecca Hamner - not Hamblin.

P. 25 - Cabiness, Charles, Junior.

P. 26 - Cardin, Robert   <u>Sookey</u>, not Lockey, Hunt.
        Consent: William Hunt, father of <u>Sookey</u>, not Lockey.

P. 26 - Carroll, John   Caty Humphries <u>Short</u>.

P. 27 - John Carter
        M.B. December 12, 1788 (may be <u>1783</u>).

P. 27 - <u>Coozy</u>, not Cazy, William.

P. 27 - Chandler, Joel   Agness <u>Leigh, widow</u>,
        not Agness Light.

P. 28 - Chavous, John   Pheby Scott
        Consent: James Mayne, who wrote a note saying that she
                 had served her time all but six months "which
                 I freely give her".

P. 35 - Crew, Ellyson <u>14</u> June 1790, not 4 June.

P. 36 - Crowder, Frederick <u>J</u>., not I.

P. 36 - Crowder, Nathaniel <u>R</u>.

P. 38 - Daly, Josiah, <u>Jr</u>.

P. 38 - Daly, John, <u>Jr</u>.

P. 38 - Daley, Vines
        <u>Consent in person by Mr. Wm Dailey</u>.

P. 39 - Daniel, Walter   <u>Jean</u> (Jane) Puryear.

P. 39 - Daniel, William, <u>Jr</u>.

P. 39 - <u>Daws</u>, not Davis, John, Jr.

P. 40 - Daws, James, <u>Jr</u>.
        (Signature - James B. Daws).

P. 40 - Decker, Henry
        Surety: <u>Hanael Talley</u>, not William Decker.

P. 43 - Elam, Samuel
        Note: Son of <u>Edward Elam, Jr</u>.

P. 46 - Delete <u>Farrar, Thomas</u>.
        <u>Fossett, (Faucett)</u>, James   Sarah Farrar
        M.B. December 13, 1790
         (See also p. 163)

P. 47 - <u>Tinch</u>, not Finch, George   Janey Short

        <u>Tinch</u>, not Finch, George   Amy Arnold

        <u>Tinch</u>, not Finch, Henry   Martha Steagall

Comment: The Tinch family lived in the Lower District,
the Finch family in the Upper District.

P. 54 - Add - George Gregory of Mecklenburg County, Va.
M.B. 27 June 1792   Elizabeth Rust
Bondsman: Thomas Williams
Married in Richmond County, Va., where the bond
is on record.

P. 54 - Grigg, Burwell   Sabra, not Labia, Elam.

P. 55 - Grigg, James, not Jesse   Martha Ealom.

P. 57 - Hamner, George B., Jr.

P. 58 - Hargrove, Bennett, not Burnett.

P. 59 - Harris, William   Mary J., not I., Elam.

P. 60 - Hastin, John   Nancy Ellice (Ellis), not Elam.

P. 68 - Hundley, Cyer (Josiah).

P. 72 - Jeffries, John S.

P. 73 - Johnson, John   Martha Toone, (widow Wm Toone).

P. 79 - Laffoon, Nathaniel   Mary Chambers, not Chambliss.

P. 79 - Lambert, Isham (see p. 165).

P. 85 - Marshall, Bennett, not Burnett.

P. 98 - Pennington, Robert   Frances Tinch, not Finch.

P. 98 - Penticost, Scarborough
Surety: Daniel D. Madkins, not Watkins.

P. 108 - Russell, Burnell, not Burwell.

P. 111 - Short, Jacob   Phebe Tinch, not Finch.
Surety: William Tinch, not Finch.

P. 118 - Add Josiah Tanner   Martha Wooten
M.B. 1 Dec. 1771   "Married at Col. Robt. Munford's
by Parson Sample."
Ref: Revolutionary War Pension Application

P. 119 - Terry, not Tarry, Robert.

P. 119 - See p. 47 for marriages of Henry Tinch and George Tinch (2).

P. 122 - Toone, William   Elizabeth Hamner, not Hamblin.

P. 124 - Turner, Terisha
        Consent: Thomas Rives, father of Joanah Rives.
              (O.B. 7, p. 415)

P. 126 - Vaughan, James
        Minister: Balaam Ezell.

P. 130 - Madkins, not Watkins, William Durham.

P. 164 - Bennett, not Tanner, Jonathan.

www.ingramcontent.com/pod-product-compliance
Lightning Source LLC
Chambersburg PA
CBHW021906020426
42334CB00013B/499